the
Kayak
Companion

the Kayak Companion

Expert guidance for
enjoying paddling in
all types of water
from one of America's
top kayakers

Joe Glickman

Storey Publishing

The mission of Storey Publishing is to serve our customers by
publishing practical information that encourages
personal independence in harmony with the environment.

Edited by Michael Robbins
Designed by Wendy Palitz and David Armario
Cover photograph by Jim Gipe
Illustrations by Rick Kollath
Text production by David Lane, Karin Stack, and Jennifer Jepson Smith
Indexed by Susan Olason, Indexes & Knowledge Maps

Printed in the United States by Versa Press
10 9 8 7 6 5 4

Library of Congress Cataloging-in-Publication Data
Glickman, Joe.
    The kayak companion : expert guidance for enjoying paddling in
all types of water from one of America's top kayakers / Joe Glickman.
        p. cm.
    Includes index.
    ISBN 978-1-58017-485-5 (alk. paper)
    1. Kayaking. I. Title.
GV783 .G555 2003
797.1'224—dc21
                                                            2002151302

Contents

Foreword by Greg Barton   vii

Introduction   *1*

one   The Essence of Kayak   7

two   Power Paddling Explained   *17*

three   Getting into Gear   *33*

four   Getting Under Way   *49*

five   The Matter of Safety   *67*

six   Finding Your Way   *89*

seven   Exploring the Water World   *101*

a final word   Great Kayak Destinations   *116*

resources   Major Kayak Manufacturers   *122*

Index   126

About the Author   128

Foreword

—

I FIRST MET JOE GLICKMAN IN 1993 AT THE START OF the inaugural Finlandia Clean Water Challenge, a tough Chicago-to-New York race that was offering the richest prize in paddle sports at the time. (I didn't compete that year and was there simply to help with the start festivities). Joe struck me as a typical jock — enthusiastic with a lot of outdoor experience — but very little of it in a kayak. Despite his lack of time in a boat, Joe finished a respectable 6th in the month-long event.

The following year, I arrived in Chicago to compete in the Finlandia Challenge and, there again, was Joe; only this time he was sun burnt, unshaven and a fair bit thinner. Apparently three days earlier, he'd completed a two-and-a-half-month long trip down the Missouri River. To state the obvious: battering your body all day, often in the frigid cold, is not what I would have done to prepare for a race billed as "the world's longest and toughest kayak race." However, I had to respect the way he jumped in without hesitation and paddled 2,600 miles to the start of a month-long race.

Joe didn't do very well that year; probably because he kept falling asleep in his kayak. But the following year, his third in a row, we both did the race again and you could see that he'd worked hard and improved a lot. Over the next eight years, this enthusiastic guy from Brooklyn, N.Y. — a place not normally known for its stellar paddlers — honed himself into one of the premier paddlers in North America. He's sharpened his paddling technique and learned to train efficiently and effectively. Through numerous types of paddling, he's gained expertise in flatwater, open ocean, and touring styles of kayaking. He's spent countless hours doing it all, and learned tremendously from his time on the water.

During a 30-day event like the Finlandia a great amount of camaraderie develops among the competitors. Numerous evenings were spent camping side-by-side, commiserating about our sore bums, terrible blisters, fatigue and other appetizing stories of the day's activities. With his humorous style and willingness to poke fun at himself, Joe always had an eager audience for his observations and stories. Joe Glickman has learned the finer points of kayaking the hard way, and now you can share in this knowledge with his entertaining guide, *The Kayak Companion*.

GREG BARTON
Two-time Olympic Gold Medalist in kayaking

Introduction

——

On the power of
water and the rewards
of paddling

IN MONTANA, I ONCE WENT NINE CONSECUTIVE DAYS
on the Missouri River without speaking. For a nonstop chatterer like myself, living in one of the most populous cities in the world — *I speak, therefore I am* — this was a rare and profound experience. With no one to talk to, a poor memory for song lyrics, and a shaky singing voice, I was forced to hear the voice of nature.

Before I set out on that long, solitary trip — my first big kayaking journey, a 77-day stint on the Missouri, America's second-longest river — I suspected that my dormant spirituality was tied to the great outdoors. Long before I returned home from that watery wilderness, I agreed with Frank Lloyd Wright, who once said: "I believe in God, only I spell it Nature." During one trip down the Wisconsin River, I took the time to paddle up to Wright's spectacular home near

Spring Green and stop in for a visit. Living and working in a location like that, surely the great architect had to have designed a kayak . . . .

A beautiful river can make a believer out of the staunchest agnostic. Several hours after starting our 12-day paddle down the Wisconsin, my partner and I cruised under a low railroad bridge, rounded a tight bend, and came upon the Land O' Lakes Bible Church, situated a short Hail Mary from the left bank. A hymn wafted from the church, and we stopped paddling to listen as we drifted. As we basked in the muted sounds, a boy with tonic-slicked hair and a stiff white collar rushed toward us. "Why aren't you in church?" he shouted.

"We are!" I yelled sanctimoniously. He hollered something back, but the current carried us out of earshot.

For millennia, people have considered rivers to be magical and holy. In literature everywhere, a river is a metaphor for change, spiritual reflection, and the cycle of life. As Rachael Carson wrote in *The Sea Around Us:* "For all at last return to the sea — to Oceanus, the ocean river, like the ever-flowing stream of time, the beginning and the end." For my part, I found the Wisconsin so sublime that after I returned to New York I immediately paid a parking ticket I had angrily been planning to contest.

Once I started paddling, my relationship with rivers deepened significantly. "The face of the water, in time," wrote Mark Twain in *Life on the Mississippi,* "became a wonderful book — a book that was a dead language to the uneducated passenger, but which told its mind to me without reserve, delivering its most cherished secrets as clearly as if it uttered them with a voice." After 77 days on the Missouri, and a few on the Mississippi, I felt that I too was beginning to understand some of what the water had to say.

The kayaking phase of my life began with a week-long trip in the Everglades. Soon after, I signed up for a 30-day race from Chicago to New York that leapfrogged across three Great Lakes, the Erie Canal, and the Hudson River. Then, the following spring I decided to paddle the length of the Missouri.

Armed with a lot of desire and precious little know-how, I started alone in early April in the very shadow of the rugged Bitterroot Range of western Montana. The Missouri provoked my deepest insecurities, forced me to confront my fears, and punished my mistakes. I began to see that river as part mirror and part sage. The "Big Muddy" didn't give me a chance to define it or judge it; it was just too capricious. Brutal cold would be followed by a stunning rainbow. Empty, monotonous plains would suddenly be graced by a herd of antelope. At daybreak, after a long, cold night, my loneliness would be transformed to a blissful sense of solitude.

The river gave me several opportunities — four, to be exact — to examine the relationship between freedom and mortality. When you're trapped for 12 hours in a blizzard without the right equipment, you have ample time to think about dying and to wonder if this particular adventure was worth it. And because each of my four brushes with death was the result of my own bad planning, or stubbornness, or stupidity, I was forced to think about responsibility, too. While the river questioned my competence and shook my self-confidence, it also summoned reservoirs of courage I didn't know I had, and in the end gave me more pleasure than I had ever experienced outdoors.

But I didn't start paddling because I was looking for wisdom or for some spiritual breakthrough. I started because I liked the way it looked. Something about the fluid motion of a double blade rhythmically propelling a boat as narrow as a knife smoothly across the water appealed to me. Powerfully. So at the ripe old age of 32, I tried it, and like the kid who hates everything, I liked it right away. So I did some more paddling. Because I happen to be athletic, competitive, and more than a bit obsessive, I gravitated toward faster and tippier boats. After hanging out with some incredibly talented paddlers, I caught a glimpse of what was possible; the more familiar I became with my craft and the nuances of water, the further I wanted to go in the sport.

Here's the cool thing about paddling: While it is a relatively easy thing to do, doing it well consistently is surprisingly hard. Perhaps that's part of the enduring appeal, and why it's called a "lifetime" sport. The ease of forward propulsion gets you out on the water, and the difficulty of mastering the mechanics, balance, and subtleties of reading water keeps you there. To refine your stroke for the maximum glide, to use the dynamic properties of water to your best advantage, to relax in and enjoy rough water — well, it's an addictive challenge, a never-ending learning curve. Paddling, especially on a big body of water, offers the psychokinetic thrills of golf, cross-country skiing, and a water slide at the same time.

Since I first climbed in a kayak in Everglades City, Florida, I've paddled on great rivers and lakes in two dozen states, including Hawaii and Alaska. I've gotten salty in the Atlantic, Pacific, and Gulf of Mexico. I've kayaked among the islands of Tahiti and the British Virgins. I've cruised the waters of South Africa, Thailand, and Canada. And it's just about impossible to pick out my top 10 trips, since each one was splendid in its own way.

Here, however, are some moments that, over time, have come to mean the most to me:

A night paddle with two friends on the Intracoastal Waterway near Daytona, Florida. The sky on that clear night was full of sparkling stars; beneath us, schools of luminescent fish sped by. It was downright otherworldly: The sparkling flashes of light streaking through the water were so bizarre that I thought someone had spiked my water bottle. We paddled through the entire night and I remained energized by the cool of the night and the utter magic of the light beneath me and above me.

A race in Tahiti from the island of Raiatea to Bora Bora. Paddling a surf ski, I found myself riding a massive swell, 15 to 20 feet high, undulating like a vast sheet billowing on the wind. Never have I felt so small. I was too awestruck to be scared; I knew I was privileged to sit on top of so much kinetic power lifting me irresistibly and then gently setting me back down.

Jamaica Bay. Many of my best paddles have taken place close to home. One fall evening, I paddled out into Jamaica Bay, a 10,000-acre arm of the Atlantic Ocean between JFK Airport and Coney Island on the south shore of Long Island, to watch the moon rise. Twenty minutes into the placid bay, I sat on a sandbar anticipating a dazzling lunar experience. Nothing happened. No moon. I waited around a while, then just paddled around on the calm, cool, brackish water for another half an hour and finally started back to the dock. As I paddled toward home, a growing, brilliant white light suddenly illuminated the water in front of me. When I turned around — bang! — a massive moon had risen to dominate the bay like the wizard in Oz towering over Dorothy and Toto. It was so unexpected, so powerful, so overwhelming that I just had to paddle to the beach and start howling.

And last year, a friend who lives in Far Rockaway, a seaside community in Queens, called me and said, "There's a tropical storm off the coast of North Carolina; the conditions are awesome. Let's go!" My friend isn't one for hyperbole, so I put my kayak on top of my car rooftop and drove to his house. We passed through some squalid housing projects, parked by a garbage-strewn boardwalk, and shouldered our boats to the beach. A mile offshore, postcard-perfect 8-footers rose before us. Because the waves weren't breaking out there, we were able to fly down the face for 200 to 300 yards without taking a stroke. It was paddling bliss, just miles from the Manhattan skyline. (I won't describe the wipe-out that cost me my favorite sunglasses and visor.)

There is a bunch of reasons why I've gone on to become a paddling fanatic, but the biggest is water and its inherent power. Remember that expansive feeling you got as a kid when you got close to the beach and the solid ground of every day turned into the soft sand of the beach? If you're anything like me or most children on the planet, your heart would quicken and you would pull your parent's hand like a restrained dog desperate to break free. Now that I have a young daughter of my own, I may not run to the water anymore, but I still feel that pull. When I paddle off and leave the land behind, heading out to an island, a lighthouse, or with no specific destination in mind, I feel instant peace and consistent challenge.

A few years back I spent a month in Oahu at a house on Kailua Bay, one of the most beautiful in Hawaii. Paddling there was incredible, but I often felt overmatched when the water kicked up, which was all the time. My friend, who'd lived there for a decade, frequently paddled miles from shore, often alone. I asked why she went so far from terra firma. Wasn't she afraid? An airplane pilot with a precise and logical mind, she raised an eyebrow and shook her head no. "The energy changes so much the farther I get away from land," she said. "The rhythm of being on the ocean is very calming; it's an instant stress reliever. And the water always feels different: changes in wind, current, swell size, and temperature." She spoke about the thrill of hearing a whale exhale before it breaches, of making eye contact with dolphins, of spying a stealthy shark or a sting ray flying by like an alien space ship. "It's a never-ending show," she said, "more beautiful at sunrise and sunset."

I thought of her comments again this winter when my wife, my daughter, and I returned to Hawaii. For two weeks I paddled in Kailua Bay twice a day. This time, I ventured far away from shore. Each time I saw dolphins or whales or giant sea turtles, I gasped out loud. One day I did a fabulous two-hour downwind run with a few local kayakers. We chased four-foot waves along one of the most stunning coasts on the planet. That afternoon, I lay on the living room rug, so tired I wasn't interested in roughhousing with my five-year-old daughter, who was looking for some action.

"Daddy," she asked, "why do you love paddling so much?"

I knew she would have no patience for a homily on the power of the ocean, nor interest in the aesthetics of the forward stroke, so I told her about how cool it was to see marine life close up.

She wasn't convinced. "You could go snorkeling instead," she said.

So I resorted to the explanation she uses on me when I ask why she likes to do things like pour sugar into a bowl of soy sauce at a Chinese restaurant.

"It's fun," I said. "It's tons of fun."

The Essence
of Kayak

—

It's the oldest, slickest,
sleekest way to move
yourself on water

WITH MORE THAN 90,000 MILES UNDER HIS SOGGY BELT,
Verlen Kruger is the granddaddy of long-distance paddlers.
He has paddled more miles than any man alive. His three-
year, 15,000-mile odyssey from Alaska to Argentina is only
his second-longest journey. I met the white-haired retired
plumber in 1993 during a month-long race from Chicago to
New York. When I asked why he undertakes such outra-
geous trips, Kruger, who celebrated his 71st birthday and
third honeymoon during that race, told me: "Rivers were
America's first highways. They're still highways, and they're
my highways."

In the many seafaring and river cultures around the Pacific
Rim — a vast area including Melanesia and the islands of
Papua, New Guinea, Indonesia, the Philippines, Australia,
and Southeast Asia — the canoe has been around in one form

or another for some 30,000 years. In Ka'Nu Culture, a history of the outrigger canoe, Steve West writes that "the canoe was to the ancient cultures of Oceania what the wheel was to western culture."

In the Arctic, the Eskimos took the basic canoe design one step further, adapting the open vessel for hunting seal and walrus in frigid waters. (The literal translation of "kayak" is "hunter's boat.") The first kayaks were made some 10,000 years ago by stretching sealskin over driftwood frames and bone joints. These "primitive" materials allowed the Eskimos to build boats that weighed less than 26 pounds — today only racing kayaks fabricated of Kevlar and carbon-fiber weigh less than those Eskimo boats. Most plastic sea kayaks weigh twice as much. For you purist do-it-yourself types, according to Fridtjof Nansen, the Norwegian explorer who crossed Greenland in 1882, the skin of the bearded seal was considered the strongest. However, Nansen reported that "the young bladder-nose, in which the pores are not yet very large, is considered good enough."

The Eskimos paddled their silent craft with an efficient double blade. Instead of kneeling or sitting up with bent legs like a present-day canoeist, the kayaker sat at water level in a small oval opening in the covered deck. During the winter months, hunters laced their seal-skin anoraks onto the opening on the deck, which made it impossible to fall out if they flipped. Of course, in the event of a capsizing, a well-executed "Eskimo roll" was essential to survival. How skilled were those first kayakers? Consider paddling in water cold enough to freeze a six-pack in minutes after successfully harpooning an animal as large as a narwhal or seal. Then imagine pulling the thrashing beast to shore in a tippy skin boat. Any reader who's done that twice should feel free to put down this book.

While English explorers in the North saw Eskimos hunting in kayaks as early as the 16th century, it wasn't until 1865 that one John MacGregor built a kayak he dubbed "Rob Roy" and toured the rivers of Europe in it. Afterward, he founded the Royal Canoe Club of Great Britain. (In England, kayaks are called canoes.) The RCC held kayak races in 1867, and by 1885 the sport had crossed back over the Atlantic to our shores.

In the last decade or so, sea kayaking has caught on as a low-impact, aerobically efficient sport. You can tell kayaks are cool by the number of times they appear in advertisements for SUVs and beer. Ed Gillet, who made the first solo crossing from California to Maui in a sea kayak, observed that: "Contemporary kayakers are merely following in the wake of early paddlers who understood more than we do about the harmony of self-propelled travel." Mind you, Gillet made that statement at the end of his 63-day journey after nearly starving to death.

While you should probably never tell a serious boater to "go with the flow," harmony is the key word in Gillet's statement; and learning to be harmonious with the water is what this book is essentially about. If you learn to flow with water, not fight it; learn the nuances of wind, current, and waves; learn proper paddling technique so that you can move efficiently, and learn what to do when Mother Nature decides to flash her volatile side, then you'll likely be hooked, and quite possibly (like me) become a full-fledged "kayak crazy." By my definition a kayak crazy can be a wacky person who needs to paddle to stay relatively sane or a relatively sane person who loves paddling so much that he or she would go crazy without it. Either way, paddling regularly has been proven to be good for your physical and mental health.

The more refined your skills and the more you learn about water, a capricious medium if there ever was one, the more you will appreciate this pursuit that has its roots in the survival of the species. Spend enough time snuggled in one of these diminutive seaworthy craft and you're likely to learn why kayaking is a lifetime sport. Kayaking seems to embody our essential connectedness with water.

TYPES OF BOATS

To the uninitiated, a kayak is a kayak; however, the term is as nearly generic as "car." White-water and touring models are as different as, say, downhill and cross-country skis. And within each of those categories, there is a variety of boats built for a variety of conditions. Kayaks have become far more specialized than they were 5,000 years ago. Here's an overview of the boats that I'll mention in this book.

These are the warhorses you may have paddled in the Boy Scouts, on a lake with your Aunt Lillian and Uncle George, or when you rented a boat from an outfitter who's been in business since the sinking of the Titanic. During a three-day touring paddle in the Adirondacks, I bumped into a fun-loving dude who told me that he and his friends have been canoe camping on a nearby island each Labor Day for the past five years. Piled before him on the dock were enough beer, steaks, and accoutrements to feed the Green Bay Packers for an evening — offense and defense. "How many trips will it take to get your gear to

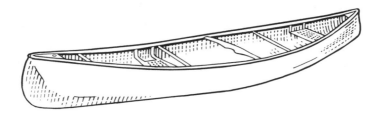

recreational canoe

your campsite?" I asked. "Just one," he said, laughing maniacally. "But we'll have to drink a bunch of the beers before we leave." For no other reason than morbid curiosity, I stayed to see if what he said was possible. Sure enough, although the gunwales were barely above the water, they managed the three-mile journey without a hitch. These two-seater boats, usually made of aluminum or fiberglass, are wide, stable, heavy, and able to hold the proverbial kitchen sink (although that camper in the Adirondacks was asking for trouble). If you're going to rent or buy one of these versatile boats, I recommend spending the extra money to get a boat made of Kevlar — it's only about half the weight of a fiberglass or an aluminum canoe and is much easier to carry on the land and maneuver on the water.

RACING CANOES

Popular in New England, Michigan, Minnesota, and Canada, flat-water racing canoes — often referred to as C1s or C2s, depending on how many people the boat is meant to sit — come in a variety of shapes and styles and are typically paddled with bent-shaft carbon-fiber paddles that weigh as little as 10 ounces. Narrow as a lance at the nose and rear, and flared in the middle, these boats are usually made of wood, fiberglass, Kevlar, and/or carbon fiber and are designed to be paddled on protected lakes and swift, flat rivers. Compared to a recreational canoe, they're tippy; however, on flat water they are stable enough to paddle the first time you try. I use a wood-stripped C2 and paddle with the single blade when I'm looking for a break from kayaking. The mechanics of the two strokes are quite similar and they complement each other perfectly. I've done a bunch of C2 races, including the 70-mile General Clinton Canoe Regatta on the Susquehanna River in central New York. If you're looking for a great aerobic workout or are interested in racing, the racing C1 or C2 is probably the boat for you.

SIX-MAN OUTRIGGER CANOES (OC6)

Were it not for the opening credits on the old *Hawaii Five-O* show, where a six-man, 400-pound canoe surges down the face of a breaking wave, few North Americans would ever have seen one of these incredibly seaworthy Polynesian crafts. The basic design has not changed in 1,500 years: The outrigger, or *ama,* an upward-curved stabilizing arm that resembles a tusk, is lashed on the port (left) side of the 45-foot canoe to wood beams called *iako.* A steersman in the sixth seat acts as the boat's rudder. I first started paddling in an outrigger to prepare for a 15-mile race in New York Harbor around the Statue of Liberty. Two years later, I was part of a crew that paddled from the island of Molokai to Oahu in the 42-mile Outrigger World Championship. With 30-knot winds and a 15-foot swell, it was one of the most exciting races I've ever done. Big in Hawaii, California, and Tahiti, paddling outriggers is gaining popularity on the East Coast as well.

ONE AND TWO-MAN OUTRIGGER CANOES

Extremely popular in Hawaii and Tahiti, OC1s (also referred to as the "one-man") are lightweight, sit-on-top outrigger canoes that have had an enormous impact on the paddling community. Built to surf ocean swells, these sleek racing boats have a rudder operated with foot pedals and allow you to paddle an outrigger without coordinating your schedule with five others. Because they have an outrigger, they're fairly stable on flat water; however, in dynamic water it takes a fair amount of practice to feel comfortable.

SEA KAYAKS

Also known as touring kayaks, sea kayaks are stable, seaworthy boats with closed hatches for stowing gear, food, and water. Anywhere from 17 to 20 feet in length and 19 to 25 inches wide at the beam (widest point), they are durable and built to go straight on virtually every type of water imaginable. In the 1950s, a German physician named Hans Lindeman paddled alone in a sea kayak across the Atlantic Ocean. While I'm a big proponent of boats with rudders, many high-performance kayaks come without them — and, in fact, it's good to know how to paddle without a rudder in case yours breaks. (The rudder or no-rudder debate has been going on for a while. Purists insist they're unnecessary; others emphatically state that not having one is like driving a car without a steering wheel.)

Its weight can be the biggest drawback: At 50 to 70 pounds, a plastic sea kayak is often too heavy for one person to lift on and off a vehicle. My father-in-law, who enjoyed paddling his 17-foot plastic sea kayak, eventually stopped because transporting the boat on his car just got to be too much for him. Had he owned a boat half the weight, made of Kevlar or carbon fiber, he'd still be out paddling.

There are also variations: two-person sea kayaks, folding or collapsible kayaks, and touring sit-on-top kayaks. Unlike a typical sea kayak, these sit-on-top boats don't have a deck to shield the paddler from the elements. Many of them, however, have storage hatches and are ideal for warm-weather touring. Regardless of how far you push the envelope, touring boats are the Cadillac of kayaks: comfortable, efficient, classy — ideal for putting miles under your hull while savoring the scenery.

sea kayak

RECREATIONAL KAYAKS

Let's say you just want to get out on the water and cruise in a stable, easy-to-maneuver boat on placid lakes, ponds and gentle rivers. These short (9 to 11 feet long), light (35 to 45 pounds), rudderless boats (without storage hatches) may fit the bill. They're also great for kids, easy to transport on the top of your car (if you don't mind hefting the weight), and affordable. If you don't paddle much and plan to stay on protected waters, this could be the boat for you.

These are usually mass-produced kayaks utilizing such materials as polyethylene or Royalex or sometimes fiberglass. They are generally wider than, say, a sea kayak or a racing kayak, at about 28 to 33 inches at the cockpit. That makes them quite a bit more stable and less tippy than the narrower and faster models, so they may be more manageable and less challenging choices for beginning paddlers.

RACING KAYAKS

Generally, any boat less than 19½ inches wide at the beam is considered a racing kayak. The lightest and fastest tend to be made out of Kevlar and carbon fiber. Used by sprinters and marathon paddlers alike, the fastest kayak on the water is known as an Olympic flat-water boat, or K1. There are also K2s and K4s, that is, two- and four-person racing kayaks. For the record: four Olympic-caliber paddlers can generate enough horsepower to pull a water skier. These light, needle-nosed boats are 17 feet long (for the single-seat model), barely wider than your hips, and tippy enough to challenge an unicyclist. Once you learn to keep the narrow, rounded hull in contact with the water, every other style of boat will feel stodgy. The other type of racing kayak, still unfamiliar to most North Americans and Europeans, is the "surf ski," a sit-on-top kayak. Unlike a kayak that you slide into, the paddler sits in a seat well on top of what seems like a long, narrow surf board. The

racing kayak

South African-designed surf ski I own is nearly 20 feet long and just 17½ inches wide. While it is quite tippy for a beginner, it is designed for paddling in large ocean swells (during one race in Tahiti, I was paddling in 12- to 15-foot swells). A surf ski doesn't take on water, so when you flip or fall off, you simply climb back on and paddle away.

WHITE-WATER KAYAKS

These comparatively short (8 to 14 feet long), wide (23 to 25 inches), boats are designed to paddle on swift-flowing rivers and are on the market in a great variety of models. They have rounded hulls for carving quick turns, with flat bottoms for initial stabling and surfing on steep waves. They need to keep the water out so most are designed so white-water boaters fit very snugly into their craft — it's almost as if they are wearing their boats. In practical terms, that means that if you can't quickly perform what's known as a "bomber roll," a maneuver to right a capsized boat while still in it, you have no business paddling on a river with rapids.

whitewater kayak

WHILE I'VE SPENT COUNTLESS HOURS STANDING AROUND ON BOAT docks talking about the nuances of boat design, I'm far more interested in getting in a kayak or canoe or outrigger or white-water boat and paddling away. To me, one of the biggest appeals of becoming proficient in a kayak is how quickly your horizons broaden. Water is no longer out of bounds; it becomes a whole new part of the world to explore. And because virtually all rivers, lakes, and seas are dynamic — shifting with the wind, tide, water level, amount of boat wake, and migrating narwhals — each time you head out you have an opportunity to learn something new about wind, water, paddling technique, and even yourself. When I did my first long kayak trip, I was struck by how often I felt I'd stepped back to a simpler world surprisingly removed from the 21st century. It was an environment both soothing and challenging. For me, that's a tough combination to beat.

two

Power Paddling Explained

—

All the reaches, catches,
rotations and strokes
you'll ever need

I SAT IN A KAYAK FOR THE FIRST TIME IN THE WINTER of 1993. I was writing a story for *Men's Journal* about a week-long kayak tour through Florida's Ten Thousand Islands. My preparation was minimal, my ignorance of paddling complete. Our guide showed us which end of the kayak to point forward and off we went, paddling through mangroves and camping on uninhabited islands along the way. On New Year's Eve we drank beer on Lulu Key with a sociable hermit.

I'd always admired the look of a kayak moving easily through the water; I found that actually paddling one among scenic islands under a vast clear sky was a real pleasure, even though I had no idea what I was doing. A month after I returned from that first trip, I read about the Finlandia Clean Water Challenge, the inaugural month-long, 800-mile Chicago-to-New York kayak marathon. I was intrigued.

I'd run the Honolulu Marathon and done triathlons; I'd biked across the country and then from Oregon to New Mexico and from California to Texas. Paddling across half of America seemed novel, but doable.

I asked an editor at the *Village Voice* if he were interested in a story about the Finlandia race. "If you're dumb enough to do it," he said, "you've got the gig." I mailed in the entry form before I could think about it too much. My next challenge seemed simple: Learn how to paddle. This was in April; the race began in June.

I ordered a surfski, a narrow, ocean racing kayak and began training. In Florida I had paddled a stable sea kayak; this boat, which measured 18.5 inches at the beam (just wider than my hips), was like paddling astride a worn bar of soap. While I became relatively proficient in Brooklyn's calm Jamaica Bay, I discovered during the actual race that paddling across the turbulent Great Lakes was about as relaxing as hiking in Afghanistan. For most of a month I battled to stay upright. I completed the race, but my technique stunk.

Why? First, I was self-taught. Second, because I was so tippy much of the time, I developed balance-related bad habits (slouching, arm paddling, and a host of other afflictions). Third, even though a few of the world-class paddlers in the event showed me which end was up, trying to implement their advice in the midst of a race was all but impossible — I'd take two good strokes, get passed by a faster competitor, and start flailing away again.

HERE'S THE GOOD NEWS WHEN IT COMES TO TECHNIQUE: VIRTUALLY anyone who can sit, direct traffic, and juggle at the same time can learn to kayak (just kidding about the juggling). The bad news is that virtually all beginners — and many kayakers who have been at it for years — paddle inefficiently. Perhaps it's the very ease of the activity that makes it so easy to do poorly. After all, to get across the pond all you do is put the blade in the water and pull. The key, of course, is to learn to do it correctly — that is, efficiently — from the start, because the longer you reinforce bad habits, the tougher they are to undo.

Last summer I spoke at a paddling clinic at the Downtown Boat Club in Manhattan. First, on dry land, I explained the mechanics of the forward stroke. The assembled crowd hung on my every word. Then we hit the Hudson River and I demonstrated what I had just discussed on terra firma. Heads nodded appreciatively; people asked insightful questions. For a moment I thought I'd effectively communicated a decade worth of paddling experience in one lesson. Then I let the mob of paddlers loose, and it was like listening to school kids at their first violin recital. You would have thought I had been demonstrating what *not* to do. Thankfully, by the end of the session most people had improved. While the basics of paddling are easy to understand, integrating the various parts of the stroke is not so easy. The keys, after you learn the basics, are practice and patience.

There's a saying among racers that improved technique is "free speed." In other words, if you can make your stroke more efficient you can go faster without logging more training hours. Now, I've heard recreational paddlers say that they're not really interested in correcting their technique because they don't care how fast they go, they just want to be out on the water. Fair enough. Speed is less important to nonracers. However, sound technique means you can paddle longer without getting tired. And that is helpful to anyone in a kayak, and substantially improves your enjoyment of the whole activity. And who knows? After you've paddled around a pond a few hundred times, you may decide to try a river or an ocean, where proper technique is important.

The difference between good and bad technique is enormous. It boils down to which muscles you use: the major muscles of your upper body, or the small muscles in your arms. Putting it in terms of a workout, it's like using a rowing machine versus doing bicep curls. Your arms can only take you so far. But put your whole body to work and you'll cover more distance and get less tired.

Even more important, better technique could save your life. Weeks into my 77-day solo paddle down the Missouri River, I set out from Pierre, South Dakota, in the early afternoon, crossing a giant reservoir. By dusk a full moon dominated the sky. It was clear and windless; the water was flat as a birdbath. I decided to paddle through the night to take advantage of the favorable conditions. By 1 A.M., I was more than just tired, I was drunk with fatigue. But I was in an area where the banks were so steep that I couldn't get out of the water. So I tied my kayak to a downed tree half-submerged in the water, lay back with my head on my life jacket, and began sawing wood. An hour later, a clap of thunder startled me awake; the moon was gone and the placid reservoir was rising and falling like an inland sea. When the first streak of lightning flashed across the sky, I saw storm clouds rushing my way.

I got moving, looking for a place to get out, but the banks were impossibly high. I headed into the wind toward the opposite shore, which was far more protected. Halfway across, whitecaps started breaking over my deck. Instead of panicking (well, I panicked a little), I put

in rough conditions

my head down and focused on my technique, making sure each stroke was efficient and powerful. The faster you go, the more stable your kayak, especially in rough conditions. I paddled mostly by feel; when the lightning illuminated the lake like a giant flashbulb, I gasped at the whitecaps hissing rhythmically in my direction. By 4:30 A.M., I was sitting on a log on the lee shore, downing a candy bar and carton of chocolate milk. I had arrived intact, thanks to my improved paddling technique. Behind me a bunch of sensible cows snoozed in the rain.

If that sounds too far removed from your projected recreational plans to be relevant, let me add that many times I have gone out paddling on Jamaica Bay or the Hudson River on a calm day, only to have the wind or weather turn hostile. In fact, anyone who paddles regularly understands the way wind and water can conspire to produce conditions hazardous to your health. In *Expedition Kayaking,* Derek Hutchinson writes that when you're driven by adventure and take your "seaworthy little boat to wild, faraway, and unfamiliar coastlines . . . you will find that just about anything can happen and usually does." In fact, this holds true for any reasonably large body of water, even the most familiar. Having the know-how to beat into the teeth of a stiff wind or scoot out of the way of a ferry that's bearing down on you turns a potentially dangerous situation into an exciting event, fodder for a good story with a happy ending.

So, having convinced you of the importance of technique, let us now analyze it. There are three basic ways to propel your "seaworthy little boat" hither and yon: the forward stroke, sweep stroke, and reverse. When you become competent at all three you'll be able to paddle farther, faster, and more safely — which reminds me: you paddle a kayak, you don't row it. Rowing is done with an oar, facing backwards. Yet many people use the terms interchangeably. Okay, it's a pet peeve — humor me on this one.

Before I get into the nuts and bolts of the kayak stroke, let's discuss a much overlooked component of sound technique: proper paddling posture (known to no one I know except me as the PPP principle).

SIT ERECT

Probably the most common mistake touring kayakers make is to sit in their boat as if it were a lounge chair. (If you have a cup holder on your deck, you're undoubtedly guilty of this.) Leaning back while you paddle is appropriate if you're trying to bird-watch, stargaze, or nap, but it's a supremely inefficient position for paddling.

As simple as it sounds, it's hard to break this habit. There is no trick to proper posture; you just have to be mindful of your body. I've seen people tape the words "Sit Tall" on the deck of their boat. Even if we pull away from the dock with good posture, most of us have a tendency to slouch as we tire. I often hunch my shoulders when I'm in rough water, in the futile hope that my balance will improve if I'm lower in the boat. Regardless of the circumstances, it's nearly impossible to paddle efficiently when you're leaning back in the boat.

correct posture in kayak

While sitting up straight is good, leaning five degrees forward of perpendicular is better. If your seat has a backrest (not all kayaks do), and you're pressed against it, you'll find it tough to do anything but arm paddle, since if you twist your torso as you're supposed to, you'll rub your lower back raw. Bending forward from the hips allows you to reach out farther — hence more stroke for your buck — and forces you to engage the larger muscles in your torso. The key here is to make sure you can rotate your upper body. Rotation equals speed; speed equals fun; fun equals . . . more fun. Before you know it, you'll have a full-fledged paddling addiction to deal with. If you ignore everything else in this chapter, your paddling will improve simply by sitting tall in the boat.

It's also important to make sure you are comfortably part of the boat. By that I mean that your hips and backside should fit snugly in the seat. If you feel like you're floating around in a bucket, you'll need to pad the seat or find one that fits you better. If the seat is so tight it feels like you're wearing a girdle, you're in the wrong boat. Witness: In 1993, I borrowed a sea kayak I'd never paddled to do a 36-mile crossing of Lake Michigan from Chicago to Indiana Dunes State Park. I crammed my lanky torso into the too-small cockpit and paddled off. Six and a half hours later, I had to be assisted out of the boat. For hours afterward I hobbled around as if I'd been cursed by a TV evangelist.

Finally, make sure your feet are firmly on the foot pegs and your thighs are in contact with the underside of the deck. Adjust the pegs and seat until you feel a good combination of contact and comfort. On Lake Michigan I was firmly connected to the boat, but nerve damage is too high a price to pay for a snug fit. The key is to feel as if you're wearing the boat, that it's an extension of your body. This will help with stability and maneuverability, and increase the boat's responsiveness.

THE FORWARD STROKE

Elegant, easy, elusive: all three words describe the forward stroke — the bread and butter of all kayakers — and that's because no matter how long you paddle, you can always do it better, more efficiently. Perhaps the inability to master the many nuances of the forward stroke is part of what keeps so many of us returning to the water again and again.

correct paddle grip

The first part of achieving an efficient forward stroke is getting the right grip on your paddle. The best way I know to find the optimal position for your hands is to center the paddle shaft on top of your head and make sure your elbows are at right angles. An inch or two to either side is all right — you can fine-tune as you paddle. Once you've found the correct position for your hands, it's helpful to place a piece of tape on the shaft of the paddle just outside the spot where your fingers should land so you can find your grip quickly (when you're on the water, it's neither convenient nor dignified to have to put the paddle on your head every time you stop paddling momentarily). When you do grip the paddle in the optimal position, grip it lightly.

Resist the urge to hold the paddle too tightly, a common beginner's mistake. A death-grip saps your strength, creates blisters, and can cause your hands to go numb. Typically, the rougher the water, the tighter one tends to grasp the paddle. When I'm in rough water I often visualize a photo I have of Australian Dean Gardiner, nine-time winner of the World Surf Ski Championship, paddling in a huge swell off the coast of Oahu. While his bottom (or pulling) hand is closed firmly around the paddle, his top (or pushing) hand is wide open.

REACH VERSUS ROTATION

The difference between rotation and reach is the difference between a solid forward stroke and a feeble one. Still, it's a concept that most paddlers tend to neglect. Here's the difference. Stand with your shoulders aligned with your ears, and with your back straight. Extend your right hand as far forward as you can. That's *reach*. Now, without bending forward at the waist, twist your torso to move your right shoulder forward. Your left shoulder will rotate to the rear. See how much farther your right hand goes? That's *rotation*. Now sit on the ground (or in your boat) and with both of your hands on an imaginary paddle, keep your elbows stiff, and rotate your shoulders. Push your forward hand to twelve o'clock. Depending on how limber you are, your extended hand will travel no more than 18 inches. That's what rotation feels like with a paddle in your hand. Do you understand the difference between reach and

"reach and rotation"

rotation? If so, light a cigar, or if you don't smoke, strike up the band! This, fellow paddlers, is the essence of a sound forward stroke.

Now that you've got a grip on your paddle and a deep commitment to rotation, let's take it to the water. There are three components to the forward stroke: the catch, the power phase, and the recovery.

THE CATCH

Holding your back straight and your paddle comfortably, lean slightly forward, rotate your shoulders, and bring your right hand at eye level as far forward as you can toward the bow of the boat. Your left hand should be hovering behind the left side of your head (with your thumb closest to your ear); your left elbow should be pointed toward the water and aligned with your left hip. Remember to relax the fingers of your left hand, the pushing hand. Now stab the right blade into the water as close to the right — or "starboard," if you will — side of the boat as you can. Bringing the paddle nearly to vertical, bury the entire blade in the water down to your hand, as if you are trying to scoop up a huge dollop of ice cream. Bury half the blade and you get shortchanged on dessert. Most of us have a tendency to rush the catch. Don't. A good stroke starts with a solid catch.

STAGES OF AN
EFFICIENT FORWARD STROKE

solid catch

power/pull

recovery

THE POWER PHASE

To make a kayak go, you pull the paddle through the water, right? Wrong. You pull your body to the paddle. Imagine that you're in a wheelchair traveling in a corridor lined with pegs, pulling yourself along from one peg to the next. You move to the peg, not the other way around. Of course, reaching out to the nearest peg will get you down the road, but if you rotate your shoulders to grab a peg farther along in the line and pull with your back and abdomen, you'll really be cruising.

When your blade is fully immersed in the water, it's crucial to make sure the elbow on your pulling hand is only slightly bent. (Arm paddlers bend their elbows like beer drinkers on a binge. This is the opposite of what we're after.) During the power (or pull) phase of the stroke, the blade is in the water for about only 18 to 24 inches. While your bottom hand is pulling, you should press your foot on the foot peg on the same side — in a sense, the foot peg is the fulcrum of your stroke. At the same time, your top hand, the pushing hand, is traveling at eye level toward an imaginary centerline in the middle of your boat at roughly twelve o'clock. It's okay to cross over that imaginary line, but make sure you're pushing forward and not across the deck. Think of your top hand as throwing a punch and imagine that with your bottom hand you're delivering an elbow to the solar plexus of an assailant that's behind you. When I'm paddling, I take turns focusing on just my pulling hand for ten strokes or so, then just my pushing hand. While the push and pull are two sides of the same coin, two parts of the same motion, each hand really is performing a separate task.

THE RECOVERY

When the blade reaches your hip — or when your hip catches up with the blade — then, and only then, do you bend your elbow and flick the blade out of the water so that your top hand is right back to eye level. Pulling the blade past your hip actually creates drag and will slow you down. Most paddlers, even experienced racers, tend to pull the blade too far to the rear.

SWEEP STROKES

The sweep is a turning stroke and its importance is minimized if your boat has a rudder. Nevertheless, rudders do break, and if you're far from shore, having a well-practiced sweep at your command can help you keep going. It is another way to maneuver your boat efficiently.

I learned to paddle on a rudderless boat, but once I began paddling a kayak with a rudder I never went back. Why? It's easier and, to me, far more enjoyable, especially in open water. Some experts like Derek Hutchinson, who paddled a rudderless kayak across the treacherous North Sea, maintain that rudders are more of a bother than they are worth. "They get fouled up in nets or lines…" he writes, "and always seem to snap, break, or bend at the worst possible time." Taking the other side of the debate is South African Oscar Chalupsky, co-designer of Epic Kayaks and arguably one of the best open-ocean racers of all

the sweep

time. The nine-time World Surf Ski Champion believes that a boat without a rudder is like a car without a steering wheel. I tend to side with Chalupsky, and not only because he's six-foot-four and 240 pounds. But even if your boat has a rudder, the sweep is a good stroke to know when you're in rough water, especially if you're paddling downwind.

draw stroke

When you paddle straight ahead, the blade is placed in the water close to the side (gunwale) of the bow as nearly vertically as possible. To turn to your left, drop your hands to shoulder level and place the right blade close to the bow in the water *horizontally.* Then, using the same principle of rotation that you've learned for the forward stroke, sweep the blade in a curving arc through the water, leaning in the direction of the sweep. If you looked at the stroke from above you'd see yourself making a giant C in the water. Instead of pulling the blade straight back through the water and exiting at your hip as you would in the forward stroke, you're sweeping in an arc past your hip to the back (stern) of the boat. The last third of this stroke pulls the stern to your left and pivots the bow to your right. Leaning into the sweep helps you turn. To turn right, execute a sweep on the left side.

Another type of sweep stroke is called the draw. The draw is useful when you want to pull the kayak sideways, to sidle up to a dock, or to line up with another boat on the water. Place the blade in the water vertically at three o'clock on the side of the boat facing the direction in which you want to move, about 2 feet away from the boat. With your bottom hand, pull the paddle toward your hip as you push the top of the paddle with your other hand. Make sure not to pull the blade under the hull — a good way to take an unpremeditated swim. Instead, remove the blade as it approaches the side of the boat. (You can repeat the draw stroke without removing the blade from the water by twisting it 90 degrees and moving it back away from the boat. This is more efficient but takes time to learn.) Leaning in the opposite direction of the draw will make it easier to move, but beware: It requires a bit of practice to get it right and will make the boat feel unstable until you've done it a lot.

REVERSE

Unless you're a rower (those odd ducks who travel backwards in sculls and rowboats) who refused to make a complete conversion, 99 percent of your time on the water will be spent paddling facing forward. It's one of the nicer aspects of kayaking; you get to see where you're going. Nevertheless, it's important to know how to go backward. This is especially useful when you need to stop to avoid an object like a rock or log, if you get tangled in a fishing line, or when you've stumbled upon a weir or diversion dam. Often I paddle backward when I'm at the starting line of a race, negotiating my way to the dock, or if I have a tenacious clump of seaweed or giant squid on the front of my boat. It's also a useful stroke if you need to back paddle to let a wave pass during a beach landing, but we'll get to that later in the book.

First you'll need to stop. Usually, if you stop paddling you'll glide to a gradual halt. If you need to stop quickly, here's what you do: Drop your hands down to your abdomen, jab your blade into the water by your hips, and push forward with your lower hand. If you need to exert more force (you rarely will), use your top hand to pull the paddle shaft against your chest.

Now you want to impersonate a rower with a double blade.

1. Instead of leaning forward slightly, lean back a bit.

2. Keep your hands low, at about the level of your chest.

3. Instead of pulling with the inside of the blade, use the face of the blade as the "business" side to push you backward through the water.

4. If you're starting on your left side, rotate your left shoulder backward, place the front of the blade behind your left hip, and push forward. At the same time, pull back with your right hand. *Voila!* It's that easy. But beware: The faster you back paddle, the tippier you'll become.

PUTTING IT ALL TOGETHER

From my experience, it's next to impossible to learn how to paddle correctly just from reading a book — the stroke is too subtle and kinetically complicated. However, had someone handed me this chapter when I was starting out, I'd have been most grateful.

Here's what I'd recommend. Read this chapter a bunch of times so that you can visualize each part of the stroke. Then go paddle. Better yet, take a lesson. Then, sometime after you get off the water (within the first 10 minutes would be ideal), read the step-by-step instructions again and see if it makes more sense. After a few more sessions on the water have someone videotape you paddling (don't let the tape start rolling until you've warmed up). Study your form on the tape, then go back and read the chapter again. At each phase, the instructions will make more sense and the principles will be easier to apply.

Finally, one great way to integrate a sound stroke in your body is to watch a great paddler, live or on tape. While I was lucky enough to paddle in some races with Greg Barton, America's greatest flat-water paddler, he usually sprinted away from me so fast that I could recognize him only by his back. However, a few years ago I got a copy of *Sixteen Days of Glory,* a Bud Greenspan film about the 1988 Olympics. One of the featured athletes was Greg Barton, the son of a pig farmer from Homer, Michigan, who captured two gold medals in Seoul. I watched the tape so often that when my wife, Beth, who had barely paddled, got into a boat for the first time, she motored away from the dock like the son of a pig farmer. Or like the understudy of an Olympic gold medalist.

three

Getting into Gear

—

What to paddle,
what to wear, and what
to pack on board

LOU, A MEMBER OF MY CLUB IN BROOKLYN, PADDLES A classic Greenland-style skin boat that he built himself. The "skin" of his boat is actually canvas; real seal skin would have been more authentic, of course, but it's illegal to hunt seal in New York City. His paddle is a narrow, single piece of wood that flares at the ends like a giant cocktail stirrer. In inclement weather, he wears an anorak, a traditional Inuit garment resembling a poncho that is secured around the cockpit. Whenever we happen to meet out on the waters of Jamaica Bay, I'm always struck by the contrast between our respective boats and garb.

My Danish-designed racing kayak retails for a couple of thousand dollars and tips the scales at 24 pounds. My mid-size, carbon-fiber wing paddle weighs less than a chunk of Swiss cheese and cost hundreds of dollars. My paddling attire is a collection of lightweight, moisture-wicking, water-repellent synthetic materials put together by the top-name outdoor-wear manufacturers. I have no idea what Lou wears under his anorak (our relationship hasn't progressed to that point), but I doubt it's got a microfiber lining. My guess is that the total cost of his boat, paddle, and other gear was less than the cost of my paddle.

There is, in other words, a wide range of kayaking equipment and accessories available, at a wide range in cost. But as different as we look when we're out on the water, Lou and I are flip sides of the same coin — minimalists who subscribe to a paddling philosophy of "taking less is more." Having spent a lot of time on the water in all four seasons, we've both figured out exactly what we need to get from A to B and we don't take anything else along.

Many of the paddlers in my club take a more expansive approach to paddling gear, and regularly cruise out into the bay carrying enough equipment to mount a covert military operation: strobe lights, walkie-talkies, neoprene gloves and booties, a Farmer John wet suit with a dry top, and, well, you get the idea. This, mind you, is on a mellow day in May. There's nothing wrong with what they're wearing; it's just that they're so overequipped and overdressed that they're more likely to expire from heatstroke than from any hazard they'll encounter in, say, a sudden squall.

The fact that Lou and I log the most miles in our club is probably no coincidence — we can get on the water faster and with less hassle than the equipment hounds. (Although who am I to point fingers at equipment hounds? I own at least 250 race T-shirts, 23 salt-stained baseball caps, and enough well-worn neoprene booties to scare a squadron of skunks.)

Before we consider what in the name of Christian Dior you should wear on the water, we need first to think about the most fundamental and expensive decision: what kind of boat and paddle to buy. There is great variety out there. (Note: I will use brand names only when necessary to describe clothing and equipment. That does not imply an endorsement of any kind, only my personal choices among — in most cases — gear of very similar quality.)

CHOOSING A BOAT

When you're a newcomer to the sport, a boat is a boat is a boat. But political correctness aside, all boats are not created equal. Ignore this fact and you're likely to be looking for a new kayak in a season or two. Kayaks range in size and shape from stubby, highly maneuverable white-water kayaks built to dance down swift-moving rivers to ultra-narrow 21-foot racing kayaks designed to glide on flat water as well as ocean swells. Our focus here is sea kayaks, from recreational boats to racing boats.

Typically, beginners will start with an indestructible plastic kayak that's slow and stable. However, once they've enjoyed a fair bit of water time and checked out the range of kayaks on the market, they usually come to realize that there are far better boats for their needs. Perhaps this is inevitable; it's hard to know how passionate you'll become about this sport until you paddle a lot.

It is possible, however, to avoid what is known by no one I know as the "I need more boat" syndrome (INMBS). First, consider:

Where you paddle. A boat you use in the ocean or bay may be too slow and stable for the flat water on a river, lake, or canal.

Where you live. If you're an apartment dweller, a folding kayak may be the way to go. If you can store your boat right by the water, a heavier boat is less of a factor than if you'll have to load it on top of your car each time you hit the water.

The length of your paddling season. The more water time you log, the more stable you'll become — which means you can think about paddling a higher-performance boat. Water temperature is also a factor. If you're a Floridian you may be interested in buying a sit-on-top kayak. Not so if you're in Maine.

Level of commitment and athleticism. Not to mention your paddling objectives. Do you want to race, tour, use the boat to fish, or just float about and get a tan? Some kayaks are even set up to carry scuba gear.

Sound complicated? Well, it is and it isn't. All you need to do is know the market and then get a half dozen of your relatives and close friends to buy boats of different types so you'll be set no matter the conditions.

TALL, SHORT, WIDE, NARROW

Since a kayak's dimensions and weight (or specifications) generally dictate its function, it is important to understand the basics of boat design.

The most important considerations when you're shopping for a boat are length and width. The longer and narrower the kayak, the faster it will be; a short and wide boat will be stable but slow. For example: My ocean-racing kayak is about 20 feet long and just wider than my hips. With those specs you can expect to go fast — no matter what materials are used. If you're young, athletic, lucky enough to paddle in warm water, and/or want to race, look for a kayak with similar dimensions. A similar boat, called the Necky Looksha II, probably the swiftest sea kayak on the market these days, measures 20 feet by 20 inches. An entry-level kayak suitable for short trips and all-purpose bashing about may be 12 to 14 feet long and 25 inches wide — any wider than that and you might consider paddling your front door.

High-tech, lightweight materials like carbon fiber and Kevlar are preferable but more expensive. Consider the Seda Glider, for example, another popular high-performance sea kayak that measures 19 feet by 22 inches. Their Standard Fiberglass model weighs 66 pounds. The Deluxe Fiberglass edition is 11 pounds lighter, while Seda's Kevlar boat is 45 pounds, although considerably more in cost. Plastic, though cheaper and very durable, is heavier and generally used in slower boats. If you plan to do a lot of car-topping, a lighter boat is a luxury you'll appreciate, especially when you're tired after a day on the water.

Some kayaks come with rudders; others don't. A boat without a rudder will be cheaper. I learned to paddle on a rudderless boat. Given a choice I'll take a rudder unless I paddle a lot on a shallow river. If you paddle in windy conditions, paddling without a rudder can be a chore.

Hatches? Most sea kayaks come with hatches. If you're going to tour, storage space is important.

So you've identified your paddling needs, more or less. Now you need to find the boats that meet your needs. One good way to see what's out there in the marketplace is to go to a boat show. I know of four annual biggies: Canoecopia, "the world's largest paddlesports expo" in Madison, Wisconsin in March; L.L. Bean Paddlesports Festival in Biddeford, Maine in June; New England Paddlesports Show in Durham, New Hampshire in April; and the Jersey Paddlesports event in Somerset, New Jersey in March. Another way to see lots of boats is to go to a local race, look around, and ask questions. When I wanted to learn how to paddle, I looked in the phone book under "Kayaks" and saw a listing for the Sebago Canoe & Kayak Club in Canarsie, Brooklyn. Quite quickly, I got to paddle a variety of boats and learned the nautical ropes. Similarly, you can find a complete list of clubs anywhere in the country on the Internet.

There is a bunch of top-of-the-line sea kayaks on the market: Necky, Current Designs, and Seda, to name just three that I've paddled. Unlike bicycle or ski manufacturers, many kayak builders are small outfits that generally produce a limited number of boats each year. A few years ago, two guys I know from racing, Greg Barton, the Tiger Woods of American paddling, and Oscar Chalupsky, South Africa's premier paddler, set out to produce a sea kayak for the recreational paddler that encompassed current racing technology. At the 2002 Canoe and Kayak Nationals in Hanover, New Hampshire, their 18-foot model finished 1-2-3 in the sea kayak division. While that may be of marginal interest to someone with a touring mentality, the fact that all three of their Epic sea kayaks are light and affordable makes them worth checking out.

To give you an idea of what to look for when you're in the market for a boat, let's take a look at the three Epic kayaks, keeping in mind that whichever manufacturer you look at, the same principles apply.

The entry-level recreational boat is 12 feet, 8 inches long by 25½ inches wide. At 30 pounds, it's light and stable. With a small hatch for storage and no rudder, it's best suited for day trips on protected lakes or calm rivers. If you don't plan on paddling a lot, don't have a lot of

COMPARISON OF THREE DIFFERENT BOAT STYLES

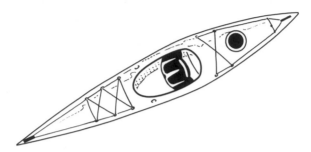

recreational kayak

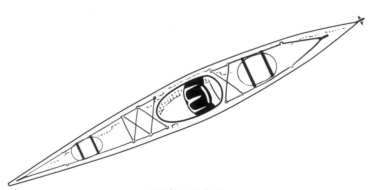

touring cruiser

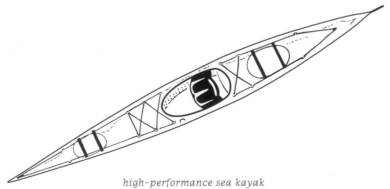

high-performance sea kayak

storage space to keep a kayak, or have to carry the boat to and from your car by yourself a lot, this is a good boat for you. This is an ideal boat for kids and smaller paddlers.

A good intermediate sea kayak is the 39-pound touring cruiser. At 16 feet long by 22 ¾ inches wide, it has a good blend of speed and stability. Equipped with a rudder (a must if you're going to paddle in windy conditions) and hatches, this boat is faster and less stable than the entry-level boat but will allow a first-year paddler to cover some mileage on flat water. If you paddle fairly regularly, this boat may be for you.

Epic's high-performance boat is nearly 18 feet by 21½ inches and weighs a manageable 41 pounds. Like the 16-footer, it has a rudder and hatches. The biggest difference is that with a longer waterline and narrower beam, it's faster and a tad less stable. Each boat I've described has gotten progressively longer and narrower, giving it more speed and performance but less stability. If you think you're going to paddle a lot, want to compete, and are looking for a versatile sea kayak that you won't outgrow, this last boat is the category of craft for you.

Here are a few other things to consider before you buy a boat:

If you love to paddle, odds are the boat that felt fine when you began will seem sluggish. That's why I generally recommend purchasing a boat with a beam of less than 23 inches. This gives you the option to enjoy flat water — less resistance means more glide which means less work and more pleasure — and, as you grow into the boat, you can use it in rougher water as well. The bottom line is that a boat that feels tippy the first few times you try it is likely to feel far more stable after you log regular hours.

Two-person kayaks are great, but unless you have a committed partner, it may spend a lot of time in dry dock. Already you see the virtue of acquiring multiple boats. If you do buy a tandem, consider spending more to get a lighter lay-up. Plastic tandems are heavy. If you transport the boat on your car top, hoisting the 100-pound craft may get old fast.

Consider a used boat. I've owned a bevy of boats and purchased only one new. Discounting the fact that I'm cheap, I have learned that a used boat in sound shape goes as well as a brand new craft. And if you want to sell it, you can usually get what you paid for it — at least that's what I tell my wife.

PADDLES

Hanging on my wall is a two-piece, wooden kayak paddle with metal tips that was used in the Adirondack Mountains of northern New York around the turn of the century. While the relic looks good over my desk, at nearly 10 feet long and ridiculously heavy, paddling with it is about as easy as eating soup with a spatula. There are two pieces of good news when it comes to paddles. First, they've gotten shorter, lighter, and far more efficient. Second, choosing a paddle is far simpler than finding the right kayak. The following pages outline what you should consider before you buy one.

fiberglass paddle in feathered position

LENGTH

Most beginners, and even many experienced kayakers, use a paddle that is far too long. When I started paddling, the rule of thumb was that your paddle should reach as high as your fingertips when your arm was stretched straight over your head. These days, however, the trend is to go with a slightly shorter paddle, especially if your kayak is less than 23 inches at the beam. Paddle length depends not only on your height, but also on the kind of boat you paddle, and your personal preference.

Regardless, if you're using a paddle that's longer than 222 cm (Kayaks are measured in feet and inches, while paddles are commonly measured in centimeters; don't ask me why), it's probably too long. I use a 218 cm paddle and I'm 6 foot, 4 inches. Last year I broke a paddle during a race. The only paddle I could borrow measured 230 cm. I was paddling a wide plastic boat, and with each stroke I felt I was pushing open a barn door. One advantageous — through pricey — option is a carbon-fiber adjustable length paddle. Because you change the length and angle of the blades, more than one person can use it. And because it breaks down into two pieces, it's easy to travel with.

MATERIAL

When it comes to paddles (and boats), I subscribe to the mountaineering axiom of "lighter is righter." The heavier the paddle, the more difficult it is to use. Ironically, novice paddlers, who need every edge they can get, tend to use the bulkiest blades.

Your options include:

An aluminum shaft with plastic blades. These are the heaviest and cheapest paddles on the market. These work well for herding elephants, but if you're not an elephant herder I'd avoid them. However, a cheap break-apart paddle with an aluminum shaft like the ones sold by Value Rite will do as a spare.

Wood. Wood paddles look good, but unless you're using a traditional Greenland paddle — the ultra-narrow blade used by the Eskimos — they tend to be heavy and expensive. A wood paddle does look evocative hanging on the den wall; in a pinch you can also use it as kindling if you're stranded in a blizzard in Montana.

Fiberglass. Paddles with the blades and shaft made entirely of fiberglass are the most popular choice. As long as the length is correct, this is a good, workmanlike paddle. The best and most popular manufacturers produce good one- and two-piece paddles in a variety of styles. I favor the break-apart models; they are easier to carry when you travel and you can offset, or "feather," the blades. An unfeathered, or straight blade, means the blades are set at the same angle. A feathered paddle is useful if you're paddling into the wind. That way, only one blade provides wind resistance at a time.

Carbon fiber. This space-age material is light, rigid, and, you guessed it, expensive: about double the price of a fiberglass paddle. But once you use one of these lightweight paddles, you'll find it difficult to use anything else.

TO WING OR NOT TO WING

Someone once said the wing blade looks like "a spoon with an attitude." While I like the line, in fact, the cross section of the blade is shaped like an airplane wing. First used by the sprinters on the Swedish National Team in the mid-1980s, the wing became standard in the racing world once everyone noticed that the Swedes' times had dropped by about 2 percent. Why the improvement? The construction of the wing provides a stronger catch at the front of the stroke and offers more solid tracking through the water. While the wing is more efficient for the

winged paddle

forward stroke, it requires learning a slightly different technique and it doesn't work particularly well for certain bracing strokes. Because I train with a wing, I also use one when I tour and seem to do just fine. If you race, you'll need one. Even if you don't race, you're likely to enjoy the way your winged boat tracks through the water.

SUITING UP

After more than a decade of paddling in a variety of conditions in all four seasons, I've experimented a lot with what to wear and when to wear it. The problem, of course, is that conditions — weather and water — often change quickly. And while you're protected from the wind and water from the waist down, your upper body is exposed to the elements. Plus, if the water's cold you need to allow for the possibility of an unexpected swim. And you've also got to factor in how vigorously you plan to paddle on any given day. If you're going to crank hard for two hours, what you wear will be different from an all-day-cruise ensemble.

The way to dial in your watery wardrobe is to buy versatile gear and, equally important, to dress in layers. If it's chilly out, I want to leave the dock feeling a little cool. If I'm warm when I start, I'm almost always too hot once I get underway. Bring a dry bag with extra clothes in case the weather turns, or in case you want to stop and get out at some point during your paddle. There are purists out there who insist that the new, high-tech synthetic materials with micro-this and poly-that are overhyped and overpriced. (After all, animal skins worked just fine for the Eskimos.) Sure, some of what's out there is expensive overkill; much of it isn't. The trick is to find a versatile selection of clothing that covers the broadest possible use. At least that's my philosophy.

Here, in no particular order, are the staples of my paddling attire:

Neoprene shorts. When the weather is warm but the water a bit nippy, these work well.

Neoprene booties. There are roughly 87 different styles of water shoe on the market. Lots are good; many have unnecessary bells and whistles. I have three pairs of neoprene booties for a variety of conditions. If you need to walk long distances, you'll want a pair that has sturdy enough soles for picking your way across rough and rocky surfaces. In warmer water, aqua socks work well. When it's real warm, going barefoot is simplest.

neoprene booties

kayaker in a "shortie" Farmer John

A 3 mm-thick neoprene "Shortie" Farmer John. I know plenty of paddlers who wear full wet suits, but I find them far too restrictive. Essentially a wet suit without sleeves, a Farmer John keeps you warm when the water or weather is cold, but also allows you freedom of movement in your upper body. A full-length Farmer John, which covers your legs, is a good option for touring or if you're paddling in extremely cold water.

Polypropylene or any other synthetic garments with moisture-wicking properties are excellent as a first or second layer. I have a variety of long- and short-sleeve skin-tight shirts in different weights, and I layer them depending on the conditions.

Hats. When it's cold I wear a synthetic ski cap. A neoprene skull-cap is good if the water is cold and rough. In warmer weather I wear a baseball cap or visor. It reduces glare and keeps the water that flies off the paddle off my face.

Paddling jackets. I have short- and long-sleeve water-resistant, loose-cut jackets. For touring, the long-sleeve version is better; for more aggressive paddling, I favor the short-sleeve model.

Rain jacket. When I paddled the Missouri, my Gore-Tex storm jacket kept me dry, and because it breathes you tend not to overheat.

Splash gear. These moisture-wicking, microfleece tops and bottoms created quite a mini-stir when they came out a few years ago. They're skin-tight fleece, lined on the inside with a water-repellent rubber exterior, and great for cold-water paddling.

Pogies. These are paddling-specific fingerless mittens that fit around your paddle shaft and are secured with Velcro. Some are made of neoprene. I prefer pogies to gloves since pogies allow direct contact with the paddle. While they work well, water does drip inside them; when it's really cold your hands can get chilly. Thin neoprene paddling gloves also work well.

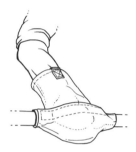

hand protected by pogie

Sunglasses. When it's really bright or windy they're most helpful. Make sure they offer UV protection, and pairs with side shields that reduce glare in very sunny conditions are useful.

Dry suits. Lots of paddlers swear by them; I've never worn one, though I would probably consider a two-piece suit (top and bottom versus the one-piece edition) if I did another long tour in cold weather. A one-piece dry suit is designed to keep you dry even if you're immersed in the drink. Unless you get one made of Gore-Tex, my fear is that you might overheat.

Now, here's how I utilize this paddling wardrobe under a variety of conditions.

ON A WARM DAY WEAR . . .

warm water	**cold water**
Tank top	Tank top
Bike shorts	Bike shorts
Bare feet	Bare feet
Visor	Visor
Sunglasses	Sunglasses

ON A COOL DAY WEAR . . .

warm water	**cold water**
Core Temp T-shirt	Polypropylene (a.k.a. Poly-Pro) shirt next-to-skin
Paddling jacket, short sleeve	Farmer John (shortie)
Bike shorts or bike tights	Paddling jacket
Baseball cap or wool cap	Bike tights
Sunglasses	Neoprene booties
	Wool cap
	Pogies

ON A COLD DAY WEAR . . .

	cold water
	Poly-Pro shirt next-to-skin
	Farmer John wet suit
	Splash gear top
	Bike tights
	Neoprene booties
	Wool cap
	Pogies

ACCESSORIES

Finally, if you're out paddling for the day there is a handful of items that you don't want to forget:

Personal Flotation Device (PFD). Not only can it help save your life, when it's cold, it's another layer to block the wind. While a cheaper vest will get the job done, the higher-priced models are generally low-profile and snug-fitting, and allow greater freedom of movement.

Paddle leash. In rough or windy conditions it could save you from having to use your spare.

Spray skirt. Made of neoprene, canvas, or nylon, a spray skirt, which fits snugly around your waist and over the rim of your cockpit, is invaluable when you paddle in cold or rough water.

spray skirt

Whistle. If you need someone's attention, especially a powerboat bearing down on you, BLOW!

Dry bags. Keeping your extra clothes dry is crucial when the weather turns bad.

Hydration system. This can be anything from a bladder with a hose, to the kind of water bottle used by cyclists, or even a water cooler that you strap on the back of your boat. (That's a joke.) The key is to remember to drink. Remember, food is optional; drinking is not.

When I race I use a 70-ounce plastic bladder with a hose that I Velcro to a necklace so that I don't have to stop paddling; in training or touring, I stick a bicycle water bottle under the webbing on my front deck.

Medical kit. There's two bits of sound advice you should consider when you leave terra firma behind:

Choose a medical kit depending on your travel destination - what you take on a weekend paddle in the Adirondacks will be different from what you take on a jaunt to the Amazon. Equally important is storing your supplies in a waterproof bag or container. To state the obvious, soggy bandages, rusty safety pins and dissolved aspirin are not very effective. In addition, make sure your medical kit is accessible. A company called Adventure Medical Kits (P.O. Box 43309, Oakland, CA 94624; (800) 324-3517; www.adventuremedicalkits.com) sells first-rate wilderness medical kits specifically designed for a paddler's destination and length of trip. They also produce a pocket-sized book with information on how to respond to a variety of emergency situations.

For everyday boat use, include the following:

Butterfly Closures (2)	Antiseptic Towelettes (3)
Adhesive Bandages (6)	Moleskin
2x2 Sterile Dressing (2)	Motrin (4)
After Bite Sting Relief	Safety Pins (2)
Antibiotic Ointment	Mini-Roll Duct Tape

All-in-One tool. These compact all-purpose tools favored by outdoorsmen have pliers, screwdrivers, a knife, a tiny saw, a corkscrew, and more. These are great for quick repairs, trimming your fingernails, and filleting fish.

Duct tape. Wrap it around your paddle or take an entire roll, but don't leave the dock without it.

Throw rope. While you likely won't use it, a throw rope is an important piece of emergency equipment. It can be used for towing (or being towed) or aiding a boater who's floundering in the water.

That's it. Now you're ready to hit the river.

four

Getting Under Way

—

On launching, bracing,
and landing – making
all the right moves

I WAS KNEE-DEEP IN SALT WATER, JUST A SHORT CAST
from Everglades City. Eight of us — six clients and two
guides — were headed out for a week of kayak camping in
Florida's Ten Thousand Islands. Although at that time I had
never been in a kayak, I offered to steady boats for those too
shaky to climb in on their own. I weigh nearly 200 pounds,
am six-foot-four, and have been an athlete since childhood.
Stepping into a kayak in three feet of water, I figured, would
be as easy for me as settling into a hammock.

I was the last one to get in. As our group paddled away
from shore, I straddled my kayak, sat on the deck just
behind the cockpit, and hoisted my right leg into the boat.
Before I could say splash, I had rotated into the water. I
heard the laughter even before I came up for air. I stood up
in the shallow water, and as I struggled to empty the boat,

which now weighed as much as a young hippo, it dawned on me that I had a few things to learn about kayaking.

Unfortunately, that was not to be my most embarrassing entry into a kayak. Three years later, at the start of the 1995 Finlandia Clean Water Challenge, I stood on the sandy shore of Lake Michigan, anxiously awaiting the start of the Chicago-to-New York stage race. Billed as the "richest and longest" marathon in paddle sports, the event had attracted several hundred spectators to the start, along with a handful of print and broadcast journalists.

When the gun sounded, we sprinted the 30 yards to our boats, lined up side by side at the water's edge. I dragged my sleek 19-foot racing kayak into knee-deep water, hastily hopped in, and landed on the water bag that was cinched around my waist. As the field paddled purposely out toward open water, I wobbled around for a bit and then tipped over like Tim Conway toppling off his tricycle in the classic *Laugh-In* sketch. I know exactly how bad I looked because I got to watch my floundering on both the six and eleven o'clock news. (Even today, people stop me on the streets of Chicago and ask if I'll fall over for them.)

There are a few lessons to be gleaned from these aquatic *faux pas*. First: If you paddle, you'll get wet. And the more you paddle, the more often you'll get wet. Yes, you and your boat are usually *on* the water, but the larger activity of kayaking is something that takes place *in* the water. So in the water you will go.

While it's impossible to avoid all capsizes and comedy routines as you progress as a paddler, the aim of this chapter is to help you to finesse some of the more common ones and to battle through those you cannot avoid. I'll cover launching, landing, and bracing, an essential part of your repertoire when the water gets rough. Hopefully, you'll absorb enough here to stay off the evening news.

GETTING IN AND LAUNCHING

Launching a kayak for the first time is a little like getting on a ski lift. It's one of the trickier maneuvers for newcomers to execute smoothly. And unfortunately, it's one of the first moves you need to master —

before you can know if you even like the sport. With practice, launching will become a fairly simple matter. Here is the key fact: a kayak, no matter how stable, is tippiest when it's not in motion. The same is true of a bicycle; the slower you go, the more balance is required.

How you get into and launch a kayak depends on what type of water you're launching into and what you're stepping off from — a dock, a bank, or anything solid enough to stand on.

DRY LAUNCH

When I paddle on my home waters in Jamaica Bay, New York, near JFK Airport, I enter my kayak from a dock that's one to three feet above water level, depending on the tide. I've paddled there so often that my routine is now nearly automatic. I place my boat in the water with the left (port) side against the dock. Then I position my paddle across the front

standing entry from dock

of the deck at the lip of the cockpit so it is braced across the boat and dock, with most of the paddle on the dock. Holding the paddle shaft where it meets the front of the cockpit (also known as the *combing*), I step into the center of the boat with my right foot first. When both feet are in the kayak, I slowly lower my backside into the seat. The operative word is *slowly*. Because I usually paddle with a spray skirt in place, I then prop my elbow on the dock for stability as I attach the stretchy material from back to front. Once I'm settled, off I go.

You can also use a similar method when you don't have the luxury of launching from a dock, but you have got some solid surface that approximates a dock — a riverbank, a rock, a stump. The crucial time is that few seconds when you are standing in the kayak just before you

sitting entry from dock

lower yourself into the seat. Your instincts warn you that this is a bad position to be in, and your instincts are right, except that you've got the paddle keeping you steady.

If you don't trust your sense of balance, there is another method that allows you to enter your kayak from a sitting position. First, you position the paddle horizontally *behind* the cockpit and across the dock (or riverbank or rock or stump). Next, you sit on the dock or whatever, facing forward. Put one hand on the paddle shaft behind you and the other hand on the paddle shaft that is resting on the boat. Next, ease one leg at a time into the boat, leaning on the paddle for balance, and slide your backside in the seat. Then lean against the dock as you swing the paddle around in front of you. Pay attention to your balance when you do this, since reaching behind you puts you in an unstable position. If need be, secure your spray skirt, and the world is your oyster.

Try both these methods and see what feels most comfortable for you. Stability and slow deliberate moves — rather than speed — are the keys. Typically, when a group of paddlers heads out, those who put in last have a tendency to rush. Resist that impulse. If you shove off hastily, you may find yourself swimming just inches from the dock. The last time I failed to follow my own sound advice, it was April, when the water in New York felt cold enough to shock a penguin.

LAUNCHING IN THE WATER

Let's assume you're putting in from a soft, sandy shore. If you've waded out into the water and are holding your gently bobbing kayak, you've probably realized that the sitting method is not your best choice. For a wet launch, the procedure for getting in is basically the same as the standing dock launch. Place the boat in at least six inches of water. (If you have an understern rudder, it should be deep enough so that the rudder doesn't scrape bottom when you get in.) Then, following the basics outlined above, use your paddle as a brace — against the shore

brace entry from shallow water

or the bottom this time. Carefully, staying centered, settle yourself into the seat and go. The first few times, it might help to have a paddling companion steady the boat for you.

Another boarding variation is the straddle method. If you're long-legged and the cockpit opening is large enough, you could straddle the cockpit, lower your backside into the seat, and then fold your legs into the boat. Beware: If you get your derriere in the seat and aren't limber enough to swing your legs in, you may need a forklift to get back out.

Launching isn't always a neat process. It may call for some creativity. One February day, a thin layer of ice had formed around the dock at my Brooklyn kayak club. I drove to a less-protected part of the bay, shouldered my boat, and tiptoed (aqua shoes aren't great for dry-land

straddle entry from shallow water

hiking) over a field of large rocks and scrambled in. I've climbed down an eight-foot ladder — one hand on the rungs, the other holding my kayak — and I've lowered myself off a cement pier five feet above the water. During a portage in a race on the Erie Canal, I decided not to run farther down the bank to put in. Instead, I tossed my boat off a 10-foot-high seawall, jumped in after it, and slithered in from the water. It was a flashy move that gave me a tactical advantage. But upon reflection, I realized that it was dangerous. Only attempt this if you're in a race — and are quite stupid.

When you travel to a new place to paddle you're likely to run into some challenging launching scenarios. Experience and creativity can take you a long way. Before you go bashing into the water, take your time to try and figure out the best way to get in and get going. Below are a few of the what-if scenarios you're likely to encounter.

The water is so cold you're loath to get your feet wet. A wet launch in winter is no fun. If the conditions are right — if the bottom is sandy or muddy and not likely to damage your boat — you can position the front half of the boat in the water and climb in. Then, with the paddle in your lap, make like a crab and use your hands to "walk" your boat into the water until you're afloat. Or, if you're paddling with a willing partner, have that person lift the stern of your boat and give you a shove. You can also go in backward if that works better.

crab walk

During my trip down the Missouri River, I became obsessed with avoiding a cement-thick mud locally known as "gumbo," a shoe-sucking substance on the bank that swallows up everything that touches it. One evening in eastern Montana, I decided to get wise and construct an elaborate path of stones and cottonwood limbs from my tent to the river so I could start the next morning without having to scrape the gunk off my shoes. In the morning, I tiptoed to the boat, held on to a stump that I'd tied up to, and climbed in the kayak with clean aqua socks for the first time all week. *Up yours, gumbo,* I thought. *I win this time!* An hour later, I stopped to put on a jacket, absentmindedly stepped ashore, and sank up to my ankles in the muck. *Screw you,* crowed the gumbo. *I always get the last laugh.*

When you want to enter your boat without getting wet, scout the bank for a flat rock or downed tree to launch from. To avoid paddling with wet feet when it's cold — a sensation akin to driving to work in wet underwear — I've gotten aboard barefoot, then dried my feet and put on my booties in the boat. Assuming you have something to steady yourself against like a rock, a stump, maybe another paddler, it's not that difficult.

Launching through breaking waves. Unless you grew up paddling in the ocean, punching through breaking waves, whether on a windswept Great Lake or on the ocean, is, well, no day at the beach. With big waves, your timing is critical. While I've done it more than a few times, I'm not good at it — probably because I shun practicing it and find it intimidating. Steve Sinclair, a legendary sea-kayak instructor, was fond of paddling during midwinter storms in a particularly wild patch of the North Pacific off Elk, California. Sinclair along with a feral group of paddlers known as the "Tsunami Rangers" practiced an extreme form of paddling: Let's call it "storm kayaking." A description of Sinclair launching through the crashing Pacific surf in an article in the *The Atlantic Monthly* illustrates the outer limits of what some people can do in a kayak: "Timing his entry precisely, Sinclair raises the Odyssea Ski (a 58-pound sit-on-top kayak) above his head and charges into the surf. The next wave breaks at his feet and explodes into foam. Sinclair throws his craft upon the broken back of the wave and vaults aboard. He is six-foot-three and weighs 230 pounds. With long powerful strokes of his paddle he drives into the next wave. He sweeps up the face and punches through the wave's roof just before it closes above him."

This, of course, is the province of highly experienced, some would say *crazy,* experts. But it does illustrate how seaworthy a kayak can be in the hands of a skilled paddler. The first time I headed out of an inlet into 8- to-10-foot waves, I assumed I'd be crushed. But by maintaining enough speed and employing a good *brace* (more on that below), I climbed over the sets of waves and carried on.

On the flip side, I've taken my rough-water lumps in exotic locales like Tahiti, Hawaii, and Far Rockaway in Queens, New York. Once on a big day — that is, a day of really big surf — on the Jersey Shore (a hurricane was stirring off the coast of Puerto Rico), I tried to punch out through six- to eight-footers in a stable plastic sit-on-top kayak. The boat at least was indestructible; but the same properties made it slow and hard to power over the big waves. After my third dumping, it became, in my salty brain, a matter of pride and peer pressure to get out: The guys I was with, who were all terrific ocean paddlers, had made it out easily.

On my fifth attempt I cleared the first three sets (waves tend to come ashore in sets of three to five). At the crest of a hissing head-high wave, I hesitated — always a mistake — missed a stroke, and began accelerating *backward* toward the beach. My fate sealed, I resorted to the traditional maritime technique of closing my eyes and praying. I rode the wave all the way to shore, and even skidded up the beach with a certain panache. According to my doubled-over Australian friend, a world-class ocean paddler, riding in reverse such a distance was next to impossible. "Really?" I responded nonchalantly. "I do it all the time."

Unless you have a plastic sit-on-top kayak that can take a pounding, you can swim well, and you don't mind getting sand up your nose, my suggestion is to exercise extreme caution launching through heavy surf. Instead, if you insist upon paddling when the ocean is lumpy, head out through an inlet or protected bay or any place where there are no breaking waves. If you plan to launch from the beach, go early in the day, when the conditions tend to be tamer. When you do decide to launch off a beach into real surf, it's highly advisable to have an experienced sea-kayaking companion help you.

Let's assume you are facing comparatively civil ocean conditions — with one- to three-footers — and you want to get out there and paddle.

First, watch how far up shore the waves are reaching. Next, note how much time passes between sets; usually it will be six to eight seconds. When you've got the wave pattern figured out, it's nearly tee time. If you're with a partner, wait until the last wave of a set hits the beach, then quickly drag your boat knee-deep into the water, jump in or on, and have your friend push you forward. Lean forward, paddle with purpose (that is, really hard without stopping) into the wave, and you should be able to climb over the next set before it breaks. The key is to act decisively: Once you get in and go, go really hard until you're outside the surf zone.

If the waves are breaking far enough offshore, it is also possible to get in with half your boat in the water, which enables you to start with your spray skirt secured. Then, if you don't have anyone to give you a shove, use the "crab" walk. With paddle in lap, do a Raymond Burr. Whenever possible, use the lay of the land, especially the contour of the shore, to your advantage. If you are launching in an area for the first time, a good map is a great help. If you can't find a protected bay, look for natural features like rocks, reefs, or an island to deflect incoming sets. In Cape Town, South Africa, I wanted to try out a boat I planned to use for an upcoming race. But the heavy seas pounding the beach seemed more than I could handle. Then I noticed that a huge boulder a hundred yards offshore was serving as a breakwater, offering a narrow path of "smooth" water. I timed my entry, then paddled behind it like an NFL running back following a pulling guard, and raced out to sea with enough adrenaline to fuel a Jamaican bobsledder on his first Olympic run. When I came back to the beach, I sneaked behind the benevolent boulder and rode a small set to shore.

GETTING OUT

How's this for basic? To get out of your boat, reverse whichever procedure you used to get in. If you're getting out onto a dock, sidle up to the dock and position your paddle in front of or behind you. Get your feet under you so that you're crouched on your haunches, and then step (or sit) up onto the dock. If you're getting out into water, brace with

bracing with paddle to get out

your paddle on the shore. Depending on the condition of the bottom (sandy/muddy vs. rocky), you might want to drive the nose of the boat gently onto the shore for added stability. This way, if there's chop or a boat wake headed your way, it will hit you from behind rather than on the side, which would rock your boat.

Again, take your time and make sure you're properly set up before you start to climb out of the boat. Beware: If you've been sitting in the boat for more than an hour, your feet and legs may be stiff, sometimes very stiff.

BRACING 101

Once you start paddling a lot you'll quickly learn that one cannot live by the forward stroke alone. Figuring out how to handle rough water is the single most important skill you can learn as a paddler. The one constant with water (as with life, if I may get philosophical for a moment) is change. No matter how calm it is when you head out, the wind, a boat wake, or a sudden storm can turn a mirror-flat body of water into a churning urn of aquatic funk.

Often it's not the weather but man that causes the conditions to get dicey. In Brooklyn's Jamaica Bay, tugboats pushing barges can kick up a massive wake. During a race on the Hudson River, I paddled from placid water into a swarm of bass-fishing boats buzzing around at the conclusion of a tournament. The water frothed like a washing machine in midcycle.

This isn't meant to worry you; in fact, once you learn the proper skills, you may find flat water dreadfully dull. However, until you're confident that you know how to react in rough conditions, fear and anxiety are likely to keep you from getting in the kayak as often as you could. And that can only lead to all sorts of social and personal ills.

Being afraid of turbulent water is natural. Having no fear — one of the more absurd X-Games slogans — strikes me as unnatural and even dangerous. When I started paddling, I had too much fear. Because I plunged right in and embarked on an 800-mile race without the skills to negotiate volatile bodies of water, I viewed chop the way a mobster views his parole officer. While I somehow made it across the Great Lakes, had I known how to brace and how to use my hips to stabilize the boat, I would have saved myself much angst.

Here's what I know now that I didn't know then.

THE SIDE BRACE

A brace is simply placing your paddle, with the blade flat, on the surface of the water to stabilize your kayak. A side brace is a rather natural move when you're bouncing along in rough water. While the

side brace

paddling head-on into waves

impulse to brace is instinctual, there are a few tricks of the trade that will make your brace more effective.

Let's say you're paddling on flat water and a menacing motorboat wake is going to nail you broadside. First, lower your hands and keep paddling — a boat in motion, remember, is most stable. Second, stay loose. Sitting rigid and upright in the boat like a toy soldier will make you less stable. (Taking deep breaths helps me a lot.) Third, turn *into* the wave and take it head-on. If you keep paddling, you may not even need to brace.

If you don't have time to turn into the wave and you feel your boat tipping, say, to the left, drop your hands and reach out at three o'clock to press the back side of the paddle blade flat on the surface of the water. That's a side brace. And the farther you extend the paddle, the more stable you'll be. At the same time you are placing the paddle out on the water, gently lower your left hip back to the neutral position to keep the bottom of your boat fully wed to the water. The combination of side brace and hip flick is your ticket to stability. If you feel yourself tipping back to the left, do the same thing with your paddle on the other side. Don't, however, stop paddling unless you have to. As soon as you're stable, make the transition from a brace to a forward stroke as smoothly as you can.

If a wave catches you unaware, brace quickly. That is, smack the back of the blade on the water — Bang! — the way a beaver whacks its tail before it dives. This quick slap should instantly right your suddenly unstable craft. When I'm in my racing kayak in rough water, I do this kind of quick, emphatic brace constantly. The beauty of a double-bladed paddle is that you've always got a blade near the water and ready to brace on either side.

Here's how it works under combat conditions. Say I've just reread chapter 2 on the forward stroke and I'm cruising along, rotating my torso for a solid catch, placing the blade close to the hull, and exiting at my hip. If I feel my boat reeling onto its left side, I'll quickly, almost instinctively, tap (or if I'm caught off guard, *smack*) the water at nine o'clock on my left hip. Without hesitating, I then transition from the tap to the forward stroke by reaching forward on that side. My aim is to stabilize the boat without impeding my forward progress.

If I paddle for an extended period of time in a beam sea — that is, with chop that hits the boat broadside — I'll paddle and use my hips as much as possible so that I'm able to brace less and paddle more. If you brace too frequently, your progress will be excruciatingly slow. If the side chop, which is the most difficult of all conditions, is severe, you'll need to do a lot of both.

Once you can quickly perform a solid brace, and also develop a feel for using your hips to keep your kayak stable, your confidence will soar in the rough stuff. Try this exercise: Paddle in shallow water to a place with a soft bottom (one to two feet deep is ideal). Then, without using the paddle, lean the boat from side to side to see how far over you can go before you're in real danger of falling in. It's probably a greater angle than you imagined. Now, while using a good side brace, lean over even farther while making sure to press the water with the back of the blade as you use your hips to keep the bottom in a stable position. Experiment with how far you can reach away from your boat (a high brace). You'll find that the farther you can reach with the paddle, the more you can lean your boat. Move the blade from side to side (a sculling brace) behind you, at your side, and up front. The worst that can happen while you are experimenting with various braces is that you'll fall in a foot of water. (And you should be able to push off the bottom with your paddle.) When you get a good feel for the brace, you'll be able to lean over far enough to put water in the cockpit and still right yourself. You'll also find that the art of the brace is nearly as much mental as it is physical. If you relax in rough water and learn to roll your hips, you'll be more stable. Knowing you can brace effectively when you need to will help you relax. Visualize yourself as a cross between a young Elvis and a cork and you'll be on your way.

THE BACK BRACE

The back brace is a stabilizing stroke. I use it primarily when I'm paddling downwind, or in a following sea. This means that the waves are either directly behind you or hitting the boat on an angle from behind (a quartering sea). If the bumps are small, odds are that once you get into a groove you'll continue paddling without bracing much at all. But if the bumps get steeper and you begin to broach (or spin out), the back brace is the way to keep you going.

Let's say you're paddling downwind with waves hitting the boat just behind your right hip. When you feel the back of the boat get picked up by the wave, lean forward, paddle a bit faster, and try to use gravity to your advantage by surfing down the wave.

back brace

Once you're on the downside of a wave, lean backward and press the left blade behind your hip to ensure that you maintain a direct line down the wave. By sweeping the blade in a forward arc — say, from seven to nine o'clock — the brace is complete. This forward motion also sets up your next forward stroke on that side. The larger the wave, the longer I keep my paddle on the water. Again, use your hips to keep the hull flat. It's a tactile thing, so be mindful of using your upper and lower body to react to the conditions. To do a back brace on the right side, you do the same, keeping the arc from five to three o'clock.

You can easily transition from a back brace to a stern rudder stroke. This is essential if your kayak lacks a rudder. Let's say you've thrown down a back brace for balance as you cruise downhill. Instead of leaving the blade flat on the surface of the water, pivot your wrist on your control (or top) hand so that the blade turns vertical in the water. Now you have a rudder to steer your boat. As you change the angle of the blade in the water, you affect the direction of your travel. This tactic is extremely useful when you need to land onshore with breaking waves.

LANDING IN A BREAKING SEA

Even if you launch off a windless beach, wind or a storm can change the conditions faster than you can pronounce "Sebastian Junger!" Depending on the size of the waves, your skill, and fortune, landing in dumping surf can scare the seaweed out of you. Rarely is it boring.

The strongest paddlers in your group should make their way to shore first, to find the best line. An experienced paddler will know that the side of a bay (rather than the center) is often more protected, with tamer water. If that's not an option, look to sneak behind a jetty, an island, or a cluster of rocks. Once you've picked a line, hover behind the surf zone (where the waves are breaking) long enough to study the pattern between sets. Remember, even if you're anxious — and you will be the first time you try this — rushing in like a mad hatter is a good way to crash and burn.

Last winter I was paddling a sit-on-top kayak on a big day on the north shore of the Big Island of Hawaii. Instead of working my way slowly to the beach, I charged a wave and found myself flying down the face. I should have backed off and let the wave run by, but I continued paddling like a man late for an appointment . . . until my boat broached and I was in the spin cycle of the world's most scenic washing machine. Everything I had — hat, shorts, sunglasses, dignity — was ripped off as I tumbled to shore. When I dragged my boat to the beach, three stoned surfers standing by gave me the thumbs up. "Dude," said one, "that was an awesome ride . . . while it lasted."

That's what *not* to do. Once you've determined where you want to land, your aim is to work your way to the beach by paddling up the backside of the waves as they roll by. Since you'll be paddling "uphill," you'll make incremental progress to terra firma. If you feel the stern lifted by the next roller, lean back and back paddle to hold your position. Then lean forward and paddle up the back of the next wave until you're within striking distance of the beach. Timing is everything (in sea kayaking as in real life). As soon as the next set rolls by, paddle as hard as you can until you feel the boat skim along the sand. Don't pat yourself on the back just yet; jump out as quickly as possible — always staying between the sea and your boat — and pull it up the shore. If a mate has landed first, he or she should help drag you to safety.

five

The Matter of Safety

—

Surviving while afloat
is all about developing
"water smarts"

WE'VE ALL HAD OUR SHARE OF CLOSE CALLS. AS A LONG-time resident of Brooklyn, I've had many of the urban variety. I've been held up at gunpoint in the subway and assaulted by a bleeding wacko on the street. One New Year's Eve, I was driving home on a two-lane highway when a car without headlights going the wrong way materialized in the night and blew by at an ungodly speed. My apartment has been broken into once; my car, repeatedly. But, while this won't comfort the would-be tourist, the longer I live in New York City, the fewer bad things happen to me. I think it comes down to street smarts: I've been around long enough to know when to cross the street to avoid hazardous situations. I know where not to go, and how to act when I get there.

Once I started paddling, I had to learn an entirely new set of survival skills to go with my street smarts. Call them "water smarts," and I admit I learned them the hard way. Unlike most beginners, who at least have a brush with the basics before heading to the high seas, I initiated myself with a race from Chicago to New York and a solo trip down the Missouri. On these long voyages, I made every rookie mistake in the book. The fact that I survived is testament to stubbornness, a sound constitution, and a lot of luck. Fortunately for me, I rarely make the same mistake twice. Intense fear and massive doses of adrenaline work wonders that way.

Ten years later, I occasionally still find myself in precarious paddling situations; that's inevitable when you log a lot of time in a small boat on big bodies of water. But in the last few years, I've had few perilous episodes to report. I like to think that's because I'm able to avoid danger before it occurs. If I am caught unaware by a rogue wave or violent weather, I generally know what to do before things turn ugly. When they do turn ugly, I have enough experience to relax and enough skill to battle my way to shore and safety.

BASIC PREPAREDNESS

In this chapter, a guide to saving yourself and those around you in a variety of circumstances, I will detail some of the dodgy situations I have stumbled into, the bonehead mistakes I made then, and what I would do now. While you may not find yourself in the exact same predicament, my hope is that you'll recognize similar situations and be able to sidestep them before the sludge hits the fan. In addition, I'll discuss specific self-rescue techniques like the wet entry and the Eskimo roll. Space permitting, I may even explain how to neutralize a loon attack, a subject too often neglected in guidebooks.

WHAT NOT TO DO

Seventeen days and roughly 675 miles into my solo trip down the Missouri River, deep in the heart of Montana, the chilling rain that had been falling for two days turned to sleet, the sleet to hail, the hail to snow, then the snow to whiteout. (Eighteen inches fell in 36 hours.) Fort

Benton, the last town I'd passed, was 160 miles upriver. The next town, Fort Peck, was 140 miles away at the far end of the vast Fort Peck Lake, a dammed-up section of the Missouri.

By 3 P.M. on this extreme winter day, the steep, slippery riverbanks were white. A biting wind cut across the barren plains. Clearly the time had come to make camp, but where? I paddled on for another miserable hour, then spotted a log cabin far off the right bank. The logs should have tipped me off that the cabin was not near civilization. When I jumped out of the boat onto the bank, my feet disappeared in the heavy mud called "gumbo." With each step I sank deeper in the cement-like muck, which soon sucked off my aqua shoes. Going nowhere, I disgustedly tossed my five-pound shoes aside and sprinted barefoot through mud and snow to set up camp behind the derelict cabin. My fingers barely cooperated as I struggled to erect the tent. My feet burned with cold. Panic was about to set in; I needed to settle down, fast. Shouting "Calm down!" didn't help much, so I began breathing deeply — inhale, exhale — until I crawled into the tent.

Crammed with snow-covered gear, the inside of my tent looked like a freezer that needed defrosting. With the wind chill it was about −5°F. My sleeping bag, damp from days of rain, wasn't warm enough to allow me to sleep. After shivering in the fetal position for three long wakeful hours, I went inside the trash-strewn, rat-infested cabin and began to jog and shadowbox to try to get warm. As darkness fell, I thought for the first time, "If I mess up here I could die." It wasn't terrifying, like a car speeding toward you with no lights, but it was sobering. The harsh reality facing me was that making it all the way down to Fort Peck would demand concentration, calm, and common sense. I ended up returning to my frosty tent for a sleepless night.

I set out again in the morning for the first of what would be five 14-hour days of relentless paddling to travel the barren windy 134-mile reservoir. The snow stopped falling, and I camped ashore each night. My hands got cracked and bloody from the wet and cold. My feet tingled from frostbite. But I viewed the ordeal as a challenge rather than a penance. Still, that hot shower in Fort Peck's lone motel remains a vivid reminder of the virtues of indoor plumbing — and of better planning.

When I told this story to a friend, a hard-core outdoorsman from Kalispell, Montana, he said, "I would've burnt the friggin' cabin down to stay warm." Good idea, I suppose, but by the time I got to that desolate cabin, I had already made a series of bad decisions. The key to staying safe during such "adventures" is prevention: First, I shouldn't have set out in the morning in damp clothes when the weather seemed to be deteriorating. Second, I should have gotten off the water long before I was in the middle of a full-fledged storm. Third, I wasn't properly equipped to deal with the unpredictability of the Missouri in Montana in April. With a better sleeping bag, rated to −20° to −30°F, I'd have slept soundly instead of having to run in place to ward off hypothermia. In addition, paddling with a neoprene wet suit would have given me more warmth in the boat and, had I capsized, provided enough insulation to allow me to swim to shore. (For more on wet and dry suits, see chapter 3.) While I couldn't endorse burning down the classic old cabin, had I carried a saw or axe I could have cannibalized some of the wood and made a small, contained fire outside the cabin.

SURVIVAL GEAR

The bottom line is that the consistent volatility of life on the water makes it necessary to carry certain equipment with you virtually every time you venture away from land for any length of time. Unless you're paddling briefly on a pond or modest-sized lake on a calm day, here's the basic survival gear you should carry, even in warm weather.

- Personal floatation device (PFD) or life jacket
- Spare paddle
- Pump or bailing device
- Whistle
- Compass
- Headlamp
- Waterproof matches or lighter
- Knife
- Food and water
- Waterproof jacket or space blanket

Essential Safety Gear

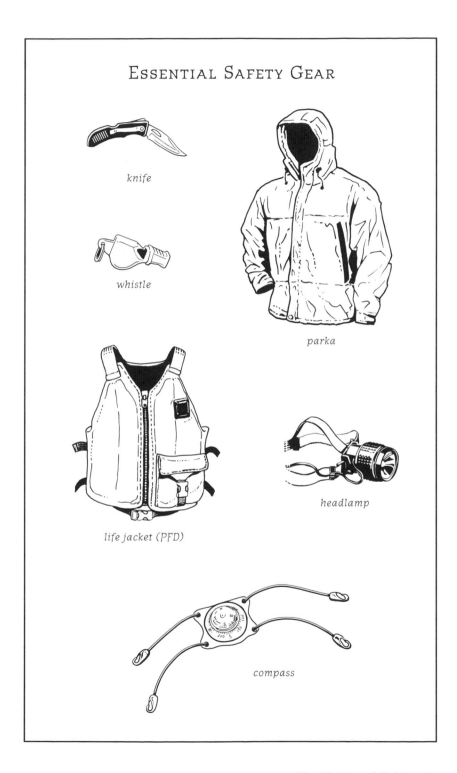

knife

whistle

parka

life jacket (PFD)

headlamp

compass

This may sound like a lot, but it won't take up much room in your kayak, and if things get really ugly, these items could save your life. Some people consider a cell phone and Global Positioning System (GPS) essential items. I'm not one of those guys. But I do recognize how valuable each could be if you're stranded, lost, or injured.

Of course, it's not enough just to carry a cell phone with you. Two summers ago, I was paddling in the Atlantic to prepare for World Outrigger Championship, a 42-mile open-ocean crossing from Molokai to Oahu. To practice the in-water changes the race required, nine men took turns paddling the six-seat outrigger. The three waiting to rotate in followed in a motorboat. Substitutions took place every 15 minutes or so, in the water. Three hours into our training session, we were a mile off shore outside the Rockaways in Queens, Long Island. Soon after a water change, the outboard sputtered and died. As the outrigger paddled off, breaking waves started to fill the powerboat. We bailed furiously until we went belly up. One of the paddlers did have a cell phone with him — until it sank along with his car keys. Who would have thought of putting a PFD on a phone? Luckily there was an onshore wind and the water was warm. We started swimming, towing the boat to shore, and an hour later we were in sight of a crowded beach. About 30 people with cell phones dialed 911 as we safely surfed to a landing with our disabled boat. I appreciated their concern, although all it got us was a stern lecture from the Coast Guard.

STAY CALM AND BREATHE DEEP

While it's important to prepare for the wide range of semi-predictable conditions you'll face when you head somewhere new, all the equipment in a kayaking catalog won't save you in an emergency if you lose your cool. Many people have drowned not because they were unable to swim to shore, but because they panicked and succumbed to exhaustion. One of the most important survival tools at your disposal weighs nothing: it's the ability to relax when you feel fear.

Here's a good example: Paddling along a sheer seawall in my sit-on-top racing kayak one summer day, I flipped. I've capsized in rough water

capsized kayaker keeping his cool

countless times. With a sit-on-top, all you do is steady the boat, slide back on, and continue paddling. However, this time my right foot lodged between the foot pedal and fiberglass foot well. So there I was floating upside down and unable to extricate myself in the chop. I would come up for air like a contorted question mark, fight to free my foot, and then lie back under the water. After three failed attempts I realized I needed to do something fast. In those dizzying moments of panic and indecision, I forced myself to relax. The next time I came up for air, I took a long, slow, deep breath and lay back in the water. Then I positioned myself directly under the boat, wriggled my foot, and pushed up on the boat with the free foot and popped to the surface.

Even if you're paddling with a partner (and you should until you've logged a lot of water time in a variety of conditions), relaxing under duress is probably the most vital skill you need to cultivate. Sounds good, you say. How do I do it? Try this exercise: Pick a day with moderate wind chop. When you're farthest from your point of departure, imagine what you'd do if the conditions deteriorated and you found yourself in a confused sea with head-high waves.

Plot a course that would get you to safety quickly. Is it fastest to head to the shore, or can you find a natural feature like a rock, a shoal, or an island to hide behind? Does it make sense to head downwind, or is beating into the wind preferable? Once you've made a decision, focus on your stroke mechanics and paddle as if you were late for the birth of your first child. Not only is this a great way to learn to perform under pressure, it's a great workout. If you're with a partner, you can take turns offering different scenarios, like wind from the west, a UFO to the east, etc., and decide quickly what you would do.

In a dress rehearsal you're not likely to feel anxious, but when the house lights go on and the adrenaline is flowing, try a simple but effective relaxation technique called pressure breathing. First, inhale through your nose. Allow your abdomen to expand. Exhale forcibly through pursed lips. Sounds ridiculously simple (and it basically is), but it's extremely effective. I recently climbed Mt. McKinley in Alaska. On my way up the 20,320-foot mountain, I monitored my pulse and ability to absorb oxygen with a small gizmo we carried. No matter how high I was on the mountain, I found that I was able to lower my heart rate and increase my rate of oxygen absorption with pressure breathing. If you're beating into the wind and feel your energy flag and you begin to fret, or even panic, pressure breathing could make a big difference in your ability to carry on.

I learned another relaxation technique from a terrific Tahitian paddler I met in Hawaii. As an East Coast paddler, I often felt overmatched by the big swells I tentatively ventured out into each day. She advised me to repeat: "I am that I am." While I wasn't at all sure what it meant, I was desperate enough to give it a go. Almost immediately, my balance improved. Why, I'm not sure. Maybe the chanting forced me to focus on the present, thereby eliminating fearful, negative thoughts. I've done it ever since. Try it and see if you reap similar results.

When you get into trouble, the bottom line is having options. Acting decisively (proper preparation, planning, and practice), staying calm (pressure breathing), and concentrating on proper technique could be the difference between a good story and bad ending.

KNOW WHERE YOU ARE

In chapter 6 I'll talk a lot about maps, but it's worth noting here how important it is to have easy access to these essential pieces of paper. When I'm in unfamiliar waters, I carry my map in a clear plastic case that I attach to the deck for easy viewing. On my Missouri River trip,

I was running scared in North Dakota from an ominous-looking storm. My trusty USGS map showed that my best option was a bridge two miles downriver. I paddled purposefully toward that clear goal and, on arrival, hunkered down just as the rain began to fall. I spent an hour watching the furious storm in the cozy confines of my concrete cover.

GIMME SHELTER

Sometimes you need to get creative. A few summers ago I was out in my home waters of Jamaica Bay when a nasty front blew in. I was only about 20 minutes away from my kayak club, but to get there I would have had to paddle across the bay into a fierce headwind and across the shipping lane. Instead, I turned downwind (for faster, easier paddling) and landed on a deserted island even though it meant I'd have no shelter from the storm. Moments after I got to shore, rain stung my skin, lightning streaked across the sky, and the wind howled at more than 50 miles per hour. (The top gusts were over 70 miles per hour.) Suddenly it occurred to me that I had the perfect shelter at my disposal: my kayak. I removed the seat from my plastic sea kayak, tied the boat to a tree, and slithered inside as if it were a rigid sleeping bag. I covered the opening with my spray skirt and waited out the storm. Half an hour later, I was back on the water.

ENCOUNTERING WIND

After a few weeks on the Missouri, I thought I had learned to tolerate the wind; at least, I had achieved a benign sense of resignation. Then, 1,300 miles from the start, I hit Lake Oahe in North Dakota, another vast Army Corps of Engineers impoundment. Oahe is known as the biggest and most treacherous body of water on the Missouri — 231 miles long with 2,400 miles of shoreline. During the nine days I was on that reservoir, the wind whipped out of the east — the direction I was headed — at 40 miles per hour or better, with gusts over 60 miles per hour. "Hard enough," one fisherman told me, "to blow a rooster into a beer bottle."

If you ever want to practice patience, try setting up a tent in a 50-mile-per-hour wind. Alone. It was maddening. Keeping a baseball cap on was a major chore. If I failed to secure a piece of equipment or clothing, I would have to chase it. (Most important lesson? Remembering to pee downwind.)

The morning I left Fort Yates, North Dakota, a bleak town on the Standing Rock Reservation near the South Dakota border, I hammered into a 30-mile-per-hour wind for three hours, covering perhaps eight miles before I was too tired and intimidated to push on. The following days, I hit the water earlier and earlier, hoping to scratch out a few miles before the wind reached full strength and the waves dumped too much water into my kayak. It was a losing proposition. Each morning, five- to six-foot waves blew me off the lake after just a few hours. These early morning paddles were like sparring sessions, with frigid whitecaps striking me hard in the chest.

After six straight days of fighting, hoping, even demanding that the wind let up, I began to understand why some pioneers in the Dakotas went bonkers — a syndrome known as anemomania, literally, "wind madness." On the morning of day seven, after four frustrating hours of battling to stay upright and move ahead, I reached my limit and headed for land. But the waves hammering the shore and the cottonwoods bobbing in the surf like battering rams made landing too dangerous. For an hour I searched for a safe spot to stop. Exhaustion began to take hold. When I finally found a beach I was so tired, drenched, and cold I could barely drag my water-filled boat out of the surf. Then I burned a few more calories by standing on the shore and screaming at the lake.

How's that for a bonehead day on the water?

I had made my passage on the lake into a contest, as if the wind were somehow against me, when in fact it was doing what wind in the Dakotas often does: blowing like hell for days or weeks at a time. The only way to maintain a positive attitude, I realized later, was to allow the wind and waves to define my path. So what if I wanted to log 30 to 40 miles a day? If the wind said, "No," that meant don't go. That's an important truth. Often, Mother Nature sets your course. Being flexible and respecting the forces of nature is a real life skill to master.

In his book *Crossing Antarctica,* Will Steger said some polar explorers succeed, often against all odds, by conforming to the surrounding forces. "Human strength," he wrote, "lies not in resistance but in giving in." While it is obvious that rivers and oceans are stronger than the strongest of men — let alone a healthy hacker like me — it wasn't until my body was shot and my ego waterlogged that I realized paddling the Missouri required acceptance, not resistance or anger; humility, not bravado.

This is not to say that you can't paddle into a ferocious head wind. You can and I've done it many times. But if you're getting frustrated or fixated on a destination despite a realistic assessment of the conditions, think again and adjust accordingly. Often I've headed out into Jamaica Bay with a destination in mind. However, if the wind has turned the bay into a treacherous mess, I amend my course to seek more protected waters. This is especially important if the water is cold.

OTHER LESSONS

There are a few other important lessons to learn from my near-disastrous day on Oahe: Never venture farther from the shore than you can swim. (Unless you're a skilled paddler on a long open-water crossing, in which case you probably won't be reading this book). The colder the water, the closer you need to be, no matter how amphibious you believe you are. In cold water, wearing a wet suit or Farmer John is advisable if prolonged immersion is a real possibility. (For more on wet suits, see chapter 3.)

Finally, if you feel you must vent your fury at the water gods once you're on land, first secure your boat.

TIE HER DOWN

During my Missouri River trip, I was advised early on by a local boater to tie my kayak down even if I stepped away to relieve myself. I thought his caution extreme until my boat nearly blew off the bank and into the rapid current of the upper Missouri. After that I tied the boat religiously.

One night in North Dakota, I set up camp far from shore. I dragged my boat near my tent and, although I felt I was being overcautious, I tied it to a large downed tree. During the night a storm blew in, the waters rose, and I discovered that my boat was bobbing in six inches of water. Who knows where it would have gone had I left it unsecured?

The obvious lesson: Tie your boat and secure your paddle every time you step away from your equipment. Spend enough time around boats and you realize that wind is more heartless than the most callous thief. Fail to tie your boat when you step away and you may not see it again.

A friend I met during my first Chicago-to-New York race once sailed a Hobie Cat from Florida all the way back to his home in New York. One day, six miles off the coast of Charleston, South Carolina,

hugging the shore

he was cranking along in a 20-knot wind, loving life, when — Snap! — his harness broke and he fell in the drink. Before he could take the Lord's name in vain his boat was gone. Long gone. "What'd ya do?" I asked incredulously when he told me the story. The master of understatement, he dejectedly said: "I had an all-day [bleepin'] swim."

In our sport, losing the paddle is about as bad as losing the boat. If you're paddling in windy conditions, use a paddle leash, an elastic cord that connects your paddle to the deck of your boat. That way if you dump or drop the paddle, you and your equipment stay in the same time zone. When I race in Hawaii, where the trade winds can separate you from your senses, paddle leashes are mandatory.

But sometimes you have to let the boat go to save yourself. Let's say you're paddling in cold water and you flip near shore. If you're unable to get back into your boat — the first and best option — and feel that you're losing feeling in your extremities (the first sign of hypothermia), don't try to swim with your boat and paddle if you're making slow progress. Abandon your craft and get yourself to shore as fast as possible. Two friends of mine were paddling in February on the Rock River in Illinois. The wind was strong when they started, but after an hour the conditions became untenable. One guy made it to shore without incident; the other flipped just 30 yards from land. He refused to let go of his kayak, and each minute that he remained in the water he became more hypothermic until he couldn't move his arms or legs. His buddy threw him a line and towed him to safety. Had he been floundering alone in that cold river, he might have gone into shock.

ENCOUNTERING BIG BOATS

My last real trial by fear on the Missouri occurred outside Omaha, Nebraska. After sunset, I was paddling toward a boat ramp, where I planned to stop for the night. As I rounded a bend, a barge train, silent and all but hidden in the grainy light, suddenly loomed over me like a five-story building, moving fast. The ominous hiss of the water took my breath away. I had been warned that kayaks could be sucked into the "vacuum" created by barges pushing water upstream, and I paddled furiously toward the bank like a man fleeing a ghost. With no time to get out — my boat was being pulled away from shore — I threw my paddle down, clung to a large rock on the bank, and narrowly escaped being sucked under the 700-ton carrier. It felt as if I'd dodged the world's largest Hoover Upright.

Let's start with the obvious. Paddling at night requires special vigilance. While I've had some magical nighttime paddles, I now make sure that when I'm out after dark I wear a reflective vest. During a nighttime open-water crossing in the British Virgin Islands, we paddled with glow sticks and a red flashing light to make ourselves as visible as possible. When we saw or heard a boat in our vicinity, we had our whistles handy and gave the boat a wide berth.

Second, it's critical to stay outside the shipping lanes. (These are usually marked by red and green buoys that form a lane down the waterway.) If you do need to cross a shipping lane, make sure you have plenty of clear water. In time you'll learn to gauge the speed of big boats and ships; early on, proceed like Great-Aunt Gertrude making her way onto the L.A. Freeway. Once you make your move, paddle with conviction. If you hear a ship or barge behind you, make sure you throw

staying clear of a large boat

down a side brace before you look back; turning your head will decrease your stability, and you don't want to flip in front of a freighter.

If you're in boat-infested waters, a common occurrence if you happen to paddle in New York City, proceed as if the powerboat operators can't see you. Often they don't. Sometimes they do but don't care. If you paddle as if you're invisible, you'll be pleasantly surprised when boats slow or swerve to avoid you. Remember, as the motorless kid on the block you need to swallow your pride if and when a big boat gets too close. Early on, I tended to go nuts, especially with aggressive jet skiers. This typically led to a more aggressive response. Remember, when nostrils flare, the kayaker automatically loses. These days I steer clear of jet skis whenever possible. When they come too close, cursing sotto voce works just fine.

IN/OUT/IN: CAPSIZING

A bomber Eskimo Roll — a move that rights your capsized boat while you remain in the cockpit — is essential to know if you paddle white water. If you're a sea kayaker, it's a terrific skill, as long as you can execute it in combat conditions. While there are plenty of paddlers who can roll a sea kayak in flat water until they're dizzy, I know very few who can roll their boats in rough seas when they've been caught unaware.

Why? Unless you regularly practicing rolling in rough water, a successful roll is almost entirely predicated on taking a deep breath before you tip yourself into the drink. In real life, here's what is more likely to happen: Splash! The suddenly wet and disoriented boater is upside down without enough time to set up the moves necessary to right the ship. Worse, most people tend to swallow water when they capsize. When that happens, pure human instinct kicks in and the flipee frantically ejects and rushes breathlessly to the surface. If the water is cold, the odds of performing a roll are even lower.

There are different ways to roll a kayak. At a race in Quebec on the Saint Lawrence Seaway, I even saw an Inuit roll his Greenland-style skin boat without a paddle — effortlessly, of course. But I'm not going to describe rolls here. Learning the roll from a book is, in my opinion, next to impossible. Furthermore, some sea kayaks, due to deck design and width, are next to impossible to roll under any conditions. To learn how to perform this cool move, you need to have an instructor or an experienced friend show you the ropes. Instead, I will focus on three self-rescue techniques that are more practical and far easier to learn from a book.

Let's start with the scenario that's most likely to occur. You're out for a paddle with two or more boaters and someone, maybe you, goes bottom up. Make sure you hold on to your paddle and boat at all times. If you've practiced wet entries in a pool or calm lake — and you should — you might not appreciate how important this is. If it's rough and windy, your equipment can be swept away in a jiffy. If your companions are in front of you, get their attention pronto. Shout or blow a whistle. The two boats that come to your aid should first collect any equipment that's fallen out of your boat.

So far, so good. Now, to get back in your boat:

1. You need to empty your swamped boat as fast as possible. The two rescuers should raft up on either side of the capsized boat by placing their paddles across their cockpits. The bows of the rescue boats should be facing into wind in the opposite direction of the swamped boat.

2. The rescue boats should lift the bow of your capsized boat (cockpit facing down) over their paddles. Positioned at the back of the capsized boat (facing the rescuers), you should help empty the boat by lifting the stern. Pivoting the overturned boat on the paddles, the three of you can drain the boat quickly. This is far quicker than using a hand pump.

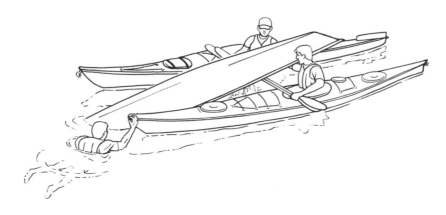

righting a rolled kayak with two other kayaks present

capsized kayaker re-entering kayak with help from two

3. Next, the two assistants flip your kayak into the upright position and slide it off their paddles.

4. They stabilize the boat by holding on to the back of the cockpit as you climb feet-first back into your boat.

It ain't pretty, but it is effective.

JUST THE TWO OF US

Same scenario, but this time it's just you and one other boat. With one less paddler, a wet entry is more challenging. Here's the best way I know to get going again:

1. Collect any gear that may be floating away from you. (After the first time you go through this, you will remember to secure everything in your boat.)

2. The rescue boat sidles up to the capsized boat and makes sure both bows are pointed into the wind. The cockpit of the overturned boat should then be flipped toward the heavens.

3. You can now flop onto the deck of the rescue boat, a few feet in front of your upright kayak's cockpit, to grab the far side of the cockpit with your elbows resting on the deck.

tipping and draining capsized kayak

4. By lowering your lower body back in the water (but still holding on to your boat's cockpit in a curling motion), you can tip and drain a fair amount of water from the boat as your partner braces. The aim here is to remove enough water so that your kayak rides high enough in the water for you will to climb in.

5. Placing both paddles across the front of both cockpits, the rescuer should now wrap one arm under the paddle shafts while holding the cockpit with both hands.

6. Now it's time for you to get back in your righted kayak. Place one hand on the two paddles in the middle of the cockpit. (Try as much as

re-entering with assistance of one other

possible to push down in the center of the boat to increase stability.) With the other hand on the far side of the cockpit, kick aggressively as you push down to get your body out of the water. The key here is to rest your belly on the back deck with your head facing the stern. Don't rush this move. Position yourself far enough to the stern so that you can slide your feet into the cockpit. When your feet are sufficiently in, rotate your body carefully and ease your soggy butt back into the seat. You'll be breathing hard. Take your time to regain your composure.

7. Start pumping the rest of the water out. If it's really choppy, you should secure the back of your spray skirt and pump as much water out as possible. Then secure your skirt on all sides and off you go.

ME, MYSELF, AND I

Okay, now the scenario you were dreading. You're all alone out there and you go belly up. If you're close to shore — and a novice shouldn't paddle into open water alone — swimming to land is probably faster and safer. However, if you are near land and the water is warm, this is a good opportunity to practice a solo self-rescue.

If you are in a precarious or hazardous place — near a seawall or rocks or inside the surf zone — it's often best to swim and tow your boat out of harm's way. If you're caught in surf, don't try to swim straight out to calmer water. Always head out on an angle.

If you're not using a paddle leash (a major mistake if you're on your own in rough water) and your paddle floats away, swim the kayak to the paddle. Never leave your boat to retrieve a paddle. You are far safer with a boat *sans* paddle than the other way around. Besides, you really should have a spare paddle lashed to your deck. Here's your maneuver:

1. Right your overturned boat and use a bailer or pump to get as much water out of the boat as you can. Make sure you're on the downwind side of your precious kayak so it doesn't get blown away from you.

2. Slip one end of your paddle under the elastic cords on the back deck. Take out your paddle float (a small, blow-up plastic device that should

Reentering Kayak Using Paddle Float

push down on boat while kicking up

hook foot over paddle shaft

slide feet into cockpit

ease body into cockpit

be accessible in the event of a flip) and fit it over the blade that's flat on the water so that your whole paddle can function as an outrigger. If you don't have a paddle float, you can try the same procedure, but it's much less effective and more difficult.

3. With one hand on the middle of the paddle blade and the other on the center of the back deck, push down on the boat while kicking your feet until you can flop onto the rear deck with your head facing the stern.

Then hook your feet over the paddle shaft just above the paddle float, and swing or slide your feet into the cockpit. Keep your weight toward the float side. Ease yourself toward the cockpit and, when your backside is over the seat, flip over and you're back in the driver's seat.

4. Finish pumping out your boat. Secure your spray skirt, remove paddle from the shock chords, deflate paddle float, and resume paddling.

six

Finding Your Way

—

Knowing about navigation
means never having to
ask "where am I?"

KAYAKING IN JAMAICA BAY ON HALLOWEEN EIGHT YEARS ago, I was enveloped by a ghoulish fog. I paddled for hours trying to find a familiar landmark. By nightfall I was hopelessly lost in the vast expanse of the bay, a tarnished wildlife refuge sprawled along the Atlantic shore of Long Island with ten thousand acres of channel, salt marsh, and open water dotted with deserted islands. When I left the dock at four o'clock in the afternoon, it was a comfortable 55°F and a bit foggy. By the time I turned around to head back an hour later, the skyline of lower Manhattan, which normally framed the entrance of my channel, was gone, erased by a dense fog.

I'd done this paddle countless times — so often that I never bothered to bring a compass. Lost in the fog, I felt like a fool. I knew that I was less than five miles from the Sebago Canoe and Kayak Club in Canarsie, eight miles from my neighborhood in Brooklyn, but with visibility at less than 10 feet I might as well have been paddling in the Bay of Fundy. I took up residence on a muddy and weedy deserted island in the bay to wait for the fog to lift, jogging in place to stay warm. It felt like it was about 45°F now and windy, and I was wearing shorts, aqua shoes, a baseball cap, and a T-shirt. As evening came on, I wondered grimly whether this was the spirit world's punishment for leaving home to avoid the neighborhood trick-or-treaters.

In the growing darkness, the familiar red blinking light on top of the World Trade Center appeared through the fog. I thought I could use it to find my way home, but once I got back out on the water I was too low to see it. I dreaded drifting into the shipping lane with its tugs and barges, so when I found another low island, I decided to stay put. A cold, hard rain began to fall. Whenever I stopped jogging in place I shivered uncontrollably. It made for a long night.

At daybreak, the fog was still thick, but I could at least see enough to make my way back to my home dock at the club. I had been out for 15 hours. Shortly thereafter I wrote a sardonic piece for the *New York Times* about why I hate Halloween, and some of my friends mailed me compasses (with rather pointed notes). I attached one to my key chain and one to the deck of my kayak, where they remain to this day. Before heading to the bay again, I studied the map and memorized the lay of the land, the shapes of the islands and shores. And the next Halloween, I stayed home and passed out candy.

BE LOST, BE HAPPY

Navigating is problem solving. To get good at it you need basic map- and compass-reading skills and plenty of time outdoors. Some people love figuring out how to get through a labyrinth of islands. Others would rather follow. I'm not sure if a sound sense of direction is learned or inherited, but I know that I don't have one. All the same, I've always loved maps and plotting trips to remote areas. Having bicycled along 10,000 miles of America's back roads over the years, I have spent many hours pondering the most scenic route from, say, Orfino to Pocatello. But compared to waterways, roads are easy. When I kayaked down the Missouri River from Montana to Chicago, traveling much of the time through genuine wilderness, route finding became a serious exercise in survival. When I pored over topographical maps in my tent each night, I was haunted by the fear of getting lost. Having no confidence in my ability to find my way along a river where every bank and bluff and inlet looked just like the last one, every time I successfully navigated from point A to point B, I felt that a minor miracle had occurred.

In an essay called "I Know Where I'm Going," Mark Jenkins says that those of us who get turned around outdoors need to chill out: "Too much is made of getting lost," he wrote in *Outside* magazine. "Many people ludicrously equate getting lost in the wilderness with imminent death — an ironic, self-fulfilling fallacy. You get lost, hence you presume you're a goner, and what do you do? Panic. Make dumbass decisions, do dumbass things. It's your behavior, not your location that cooks your goose."

He makes a valuable point. When you are making your way through unfamiliar waters or woods, concentration, patience, and solid map skills are extremely important, especially when you're traveling alone. But if you do get lost — and you will if you spend enough time out there — you need to remain calm to turn that visceral feeling of confusion into what Jenkins calls "a temporary affliction with minor consequences."

His comment reminded me of a story my mother told me about her Aunt Rifka, who typically arrived at get-togethers hours late. The nervous members in the family — 99 percent of the adults — would panic. Rifka spoke little English and never carried enough money. When she finally walked through the door they would all pounce on her. "Where in God's name were you?"

"I got lost," she'd say. "But I met some wonderful people."

Old Rifka may have had her head in the clouds, but she had the perfect mentality to lead a long-distance kayak trip. To her, being lost was not a failure but an adventure.

WATER, WATER EVERYWHERE

As a fledgling paddler, I was struck by the fact that there are precious few signs out on the water. When I cycled, even on the most deserted roads in Nevada, it was fairly obvious which way to go. If I did get lost, a sign or person or some landmark eventually appeared to set me straight. Even hiking in the backcountry there were trails and plenty of natural features — a lake, a mountain, railroad tracks — to orient myself if I lost contact with where I was on the map.

But I discovered that navigating on the water required a new level of geographical sophistication. Words were out; I had to learn to read the land. Unless you pass a bridge, marina, or town along the water, one bay looks like the next. That bend in the river could have been any of the last few you passed. In unfamiliar coastal territory, you can head off a beach, paddle in one direction for an hour, turn around and head back, and still have a truly difficult time finding the place where you launched. This, mind you, is on a clear day. Now when I head out on a new body of water, I paddle out a short distance and turn around to take a mental snapshot of the shore. I'm looking for a distinct feature like a building (I note its color and size) or channel marker (most are numbered) — something that's solidly fixed in place that will tell me that I'm back where I started.

In a kayak, sitting so low on the water, it's hard to get the perspective to see whether you're still on course. In the woods you can often climb to high ground to see where you've come from or where you are going. In fact, that's what I did a few times on the Missouri River (after tying up my boat securely, of course): I went ashore and climbed up a bluff for a look around. And since water breeds fog, especially on large bodies of water, you have to be prepared to lose even the perspective you do have. (If any of you need a compass, let me know since I have quite a few extras lying around.)

To add to your "nav" concerns, there tend to be far fewer people out on the water to help you if you get temporarily misplaced. Heading across Fort Peck Reservoir, an enormous body of water in Montana with countless dead-end bays, I didn't see another soul for a week. (I studied my map like a law student cramming for the bar exam.) Earlier in my trip, I was on another, smaller lake and failed to see where the river turned sharply to the west. I blundered around until I was completely confused. Then I spotted a farm on the far shore. Bingo! I'll paddle over, I thought, and ask directions; they might even take pity on a poor paddler and offer me lunch and, if I'm lucky, their daughter, who'll turn out to be an Olympic-caliber kayaker. After paddling several miles out of my way, I went ashore, and felt like I'd stepped onto the set of the *Twilight Zone*. The house was so weathered it seemed as if no one had lived there since the Eisenhower Administration. The deserted property was littered with rusted vehicles, some of them with trees growing through their bodies. No help there.

I mention all these potential pitfalls to let you know that navigating on a sprawling body of water takes some getting used to. In the beginning it's natural to feel shaky. Don't despair. Think like Aunt Rifka; welcome the challenge. Over time, even if you're like me, you'll see that all you need to find your way is a good topo map and patience (a GPS, cell phone, and blood hound are optional).

MAP ME

My map fetish started in 1988 when I cycled across America, and it intensified during the three long bicycle tours that followed. And when I paddled down the Missouri in 1995, I had little control over a nearly compulsive need to read maps, the more detailed the better. As my addiction grew stronger, I'd catch myself whiling away precious time, tracing the thin blue line of a river from its source to mouth, or scanning the emptier spots on the map for tiny towns with evocative names.

Unless you're paddling in a pond, navigating a big body of water requires a good marine map (known as a chart) or a topographic map from the United States Geological Survey (USGS) with enough detail to get you down the watery road. Each map has its own scale, such as 1:80,000, which means 1 inch on the chart equals 80,000 inches in the real world (or 1.1 nautical miles in real distance). For coastal paddling a scale of 1:50,000 or more should be fine. (The larger the scale of the chart, the smaller the area it will cover.) The more remote the area, the greater the detail you'll need. Charts tell you almost anything you could want to know about a body of water, like where the marinas and fish hatcheries are, as well as much smaller features, like the buoys that mark channels. They also give water depths, although kayakers don't often need to worry about that.

Topo maps, which I used on the Missouri, work well for rivers in the back country. The USGS 7.5 minute maps show great detail, and their tiny squiggly brown contour lines usually indicate variations in elevation of 10 or 20 feet. So, the more closely spaced the lines, the steeper the contour; the more space between the lines, the more level the terrain. That way, reading the map you can tell whether a riverbank is a

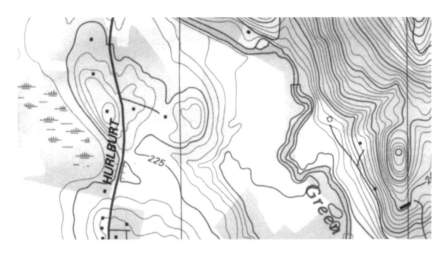

topo map shows contours of the riverbank

steep cliff or a gentle slope. Knowing the lay of the land might not seem important when you're eyeing the map in your living room, but when you're in the bush, identifying distinct geological features — mountain, cliff, gorge — can be as valuable as reading any road sign.

Here's a good example of extreme on-the-job training. Halfway across Montana on the Missouri, I focused on getting around a peninsula called UL Bend, located at the confluence of the Missouri and Musselshell Rivers. Because huge stretches of the Missouri in central

Montana resemble what's ahead and behind, much of the time I had only an approximate idea of where I was at any given hour. Considering my lack of experience and so-so sense of direction, I approached major navigational decisions with anxiety bordering on terror. Out there, I would have killed for a road sign in Swahili.

To a traveler on foot, UL Bend is a mile across; on the water, it's 10 miles or more to get around. Seen from above or on a map, the curve in the river is obvious. From kayak level on the water, however, the bend is so gradual, the land so similar, that it is easy to get confused. To head down the Musselshell, which joins the Mighty Mo at the elbow of the bend, and not around the peninsula, would be the equivalent of missing the freeway exit to Los Angeles and ending up in San Diego. Except you wouldn't see any signs until you arrived in the wrong city.

Knowing what I know now, navigating around UL Bend seems like no big deal. But back then I practiced a primitive and paranoid form of navigation. I hugged the left bank and stole glances at my compass all day. I did the right thing by following the river bank, but instead of staring at my compass like a groupie would a rock star, I should have picked a distinct point in the distance (known in orienteering as an "attack point") and focused on that. Once I made it there, I should have keyed off another recognizable feature and repeated the process.

Instead I considered getting out and walking across the peninsula, but the land was too fractured and my load too bulky. So I paddled on, resenting the "extra" mileage as if I had been denied some inalienable right. Late in the day, when the little quivering red needle of my hand-held compass turned north away from the beckoning mouth of the southerly Musselshell, I knew I was headed in the right direction. I felt a surge of relief and boost of confidence that left me almost giddy. I was ecstatic because I wasn't lost — kind of like a golfer celebrating not missing the ball on the tee. Had I wanted to soothe my troubled soul, I could have hiked to a high point, map and compass in hand, figured out where I was, and continued on. By maintaining "contact" with the map, you virtually eliminate that sickening feeling of uncertainty when you don't really know where you are and when it's possible that every paddle stroke is taking you even farther in a wrong direction.

Jenkins says that maps are "the promise of discovery, geography of odysseys to come." While that may be a bit grandiose, it's true. The more you scrutinize a good map, the more that's revealed. If you study this coded document carefully, weeks before you head out on a trip, as well as the night before you set out on the water, you'll find that matching the features on the map with those on land gets easier and easier. Ultimately, experience and common sense are your essential guides.

Finally, maps, like the proverbial powder, must be kept dry. I store mine in two large zip-top bags that I attach to my fore-deck. There are also specially made transparent map carriers that work well. Some people cut their maps down to the area they intend to travel and cover each side with a self-adhesive, transparent, waterproof covering, but I like to know where I am in a larger context, so I usually take the whole map. On my trip on the Missouri, I mailed maps home when I finished with them. They're better than photographs in helping me remember the details of my epic and not-so-epic voyages.

COMPASS TIME

Being able to read and interpret a map is the biggest skill you'll need in your paddling career, once you venture beyond your home pond or harbor. In most cases, to be an effective navigator from the seat of a kayak you just need to know where you're going, the direction you have to go, and your basic speed.

But there will be times when a compass is not merely helpful but essential. In 1993, I lined up for a 45-mile race on Lake Ontario from Hamilton, Canada, to Niagara-on-the-Lake, New York. The sky was gray and overcast, and because we were going to be at least six miles from shore, I was anxious about fighting rough water all day. An hour into the race, the wind died, and the lake, which had been rocking, settled into an eerie calm. A light rain fell. Visibility declined to about zero; the only way to navigate was by compass. Lake Ontario was shrouded in mist and undulated like a giant waterbed, seeming as vast as an ocean. For seven hours I paddled through the gentle, rhythmic swells and thick fog without the benefit of a single visual clue to where I was going. When I hit the far shore, the channel leading to the finish appeared like an apparition. It sounds funny, but I felt real gratitude toward the little plastic directional device that had guided me across that immense inland sea.

While you can get fancy with a compass — there's even a sport called "orienteering," which is sort of the X-Game of navigation — you can get by without knowing how to triangulate a position or understanding transits. The primary skill you'll need to know is how to take a simple bearing, to use your compass to establish a reassuring line to follow when fog, darkness, and indecision conspire to keep you from your destination.

Here's how you take a bearing (see illustrations on page 98):

1. With the straight edge of your handheld compass, line up your intended route of travel from point A to B on your map. For example: If you're crossing a large reservoir on a river, line the ruler edge of your compass from where you'll start to the finish.

2. Now turn the dial of the compass housing until the lines marked N & S (for north and south) are parallel with the north-south lines on your map. (It's important that the N on your compass is pointing the direction that north is shown on your map.)

3. Now the tricky part — correcting for what's known in the business of navigation as *declination*. That is the magnetic variation between the vertical lines on your map, called geographic (or true) north, and the actual direction your compass needle points when you're out in the field. Accounting for the difference is quite simple since declination will usually be shown at the bottom of your map or chart, if it's of USGS issue. The difference is noted in degrees east or west of the true north. (Often there's no need to correct for declination.) To help me remember which way to turn my dial, I use the adage: east is least (subtract) or west is best (add).

4. Turn the dial on the compass until the magnetic needle lines up with the fixed arrow on the compass housing. Voilà! That should give you the correct bearing to the perfect picnic or campsite.

USING A COMPASS

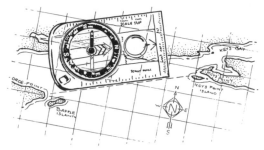

line up straight edge of compass with intended route

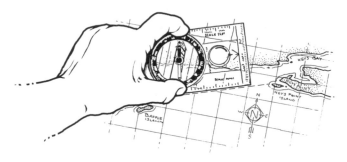

turn compass dial until N & S lines are parallel with N & S lines on map

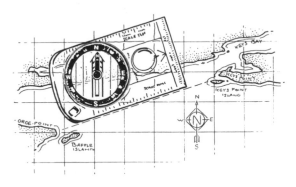

turn compass dial until magnetic needle lines up with fixed needle

Here are a few additional things to keep in mind:

A good navigator always trusts the compass.

Secure your compass to your boat or life jacket. Compasses, like GPSs, tend to float away (or sink). If you're going on a multi-day trip, taking two compasses is a good idea.

If you're paddling in a fog or at night, you'll have to pay careful attention to your bearing; however, if you site a visual reference on route — a bluff, a power plant, or an island — aim for that and you'll be able to look around instead of at your compass. Be careful what you pick, though. On Lake Michigan I once mistakenly used a supertanker as a reference point. They're easy to see miles away but they move. Similarly, don't confuse compass directions with sunlight directions. The sun moves, too.

GLOBAL POSITIONING SYSTEMS

Some people consider the GPS the best thing to happen in the world of navigation since the sextant. Lightweight, compact, affordable, and astonishingly accurate, they are incredible tools. You can download a USGS topography map into one of these lightweight gizmos, program the coordinates of a trip you want to take, and then follow the little directional arrow the way you would painted footprints in a theme park. (Look Mom, no map!)

Four years ago, I did a 36-mile crossing of the Saint Lawrence Seaway in northern Quebec. Visibility was poor, so navigating by compass was essential. What we failed to account for, however, was that we were being pushed downstream. When we hit the opposite shore five hours later, we were two miles farther south than we'd planned. The next year I did the crossing with a GPS mounted on the deck on my kayak. After programming in the coordinates of the start and finish, all I had to do was follow the arrow that led me like a seeing-eye dog to the finish line. Since the GPS gives you miles per hour, it's a great tool for a racer. By tweaking your stroke, you can see how the adjustments you make affect your speed.

However, if you lose your GPS, if its little batteries die, or you experience some other mechanical snafu, you may be up the proverbial creek sans paddle. I own a GPS, but I rarely use it. Partly that's because I go paddling to escape technology; partly that's because I've seen too many people muttering profanities when their GPS malfunctions. And the rest is because I'm too lazy to replace the batteries. In addition, sometimes the satellite signal is affected by the lay of the land (a dense forest or canyon will obscure the signal). So take a GPS along if you like — it may prove to be an invaluable addition to your navigational arsenal if you're running a remote river in the Yukon (or fogbound on the coast of Connecticut, for that matter) — but make sure you know how to read a map and use a compass. Because when your GPS goes down, you may have to start thinking about sending up smoke signals.

seven

Exploring the Water World

—

For touring, turn
your kayak into a home
away from home

ON A FRIGID AFTERNOON IN FEBRUARY, I WAS RUNNING
nowhere on a treadmill in a Brooklyn gym, chatting with
George, a bald, bearded banker who somehow maintained his
tan in the dead of winter.

"You're doing what?" he asked.

"I'm going to kayak from Montana to New York."

"Alone?"

"I'll be solo for the first 2,600 miles to Chicago." I acted
as nonchalant as possible. "From there I'll hook up with a 30-
day race and paddle to New York City."

He paused to take it all in. "I've got two things to say:
Don't get killed. And I hate the Chicago Bulls."

Except for his comment about Michael Jordan's Bulls,
slayers of his beloved Knicks, George's reaction was fairly
typical. When I told friends about the trip, most said I was

nuts to paddle solo in the wilds of Montana. Later, when folks out West learned that I was from New York City, they said I was crazy to live in such a dangerous place. But once I decided to follow the route of the Lewis and Clark expedition on the Missouri — only in reverse and downriver — from Red Rock, Montana, to Saint Charles, Missouri, I thought of little else as I trained in my cramped gym that winter of 1994.

When I traced the thin blue line of the Missouri on my map undulating in all four directions across America, I had my own doubts. That was my first year in the sport and I had done a lot of paddling, but never in the wilderness and never alone. Did I have the white-water skills to handle the Beaverhead and Jefferson, the tributaries I'd travel to get to the headwaters of the Missouri? Did I have the chops to handle the sub-zero weather and spring snowstorms that hit Montana? The one time I had camped in the snow in the Adirondack Mountains, my brother, my dog, and I almost froze to death. How would I manage the relentless wind and waves on the reservoirs in Montana and the Dakotas? What about those big barge wakes on the lower Missouri where the commercial traffic was so heavy? What gear should I take? How much food could I carry? How would I manage long stretches of wilderness between towns?

Near the end of my workout, George returned. He motioned for me to remove my walkman. I figured he had important advice about my challenging trip. "You'll be away for four months?"

I held up three fingers.

"How many rolls of toilet paper are you going to take?"

Clearly, I would need to seek the help I needed outside my usual social circles.

Alan Kesselheim, who's logged over 10,000 miles in his canoe, writes in *The Wilderness Paddler's Handbook:* "If I had to come up with a pithy summary of my canoe tripping philosophy, it would be something like this: "Get in the boat and go! Things will work out. If they don't, figure out how to adapt . . . I'd go so far as to say that trips are nine-tenths inspiration and one-tenth information."

Since this is the way I like to approach life, as well as trips, I agree with him. However, Kesselheim is also quick to admit that he has learned a lot of tricks about tripping over the years, often in the course of screwing up the first time around. Me too. In fact, when I look back at how untested I was at the start of my Missouri trip, it is a minor miracle I made it home in one piece. So in this chapter, I'll offer guidelines for planning a trip, and some advice about what to take and what to leave. And what to expect. This way, you can avoid the mistakes I made and concentrate on making your own.

IN THE BEGINNING

When I was growing up in Rockland County, north of New York City, a fanatical cyclist named Gary lived in my neighborhood. One evening he came tearing around the corner like Paul Revere. "Where ya coming from?" I shouted. "Philadelphia!" he replied without slowing down. Back then I didn't know where Philly was, but I knew it was far away. The next summer, he cycled across America. At age 10, I thought I was hot stuff on my banana bike with slick tires, but such a journey was unimaginable. Twenty years later, in 1988, I rode from Santa Barbara, California, to New York on an ordinary lightweight 10-speed. That 42-day, 3,400-mile ride inspired my next month-long trip out West; and that led to another and another.

Some journeys are long-simmering; others are born in a flash. One hot afternoon, my friend Joe Weight was stuck in New York's Lincoln Tunnel. He was so exasperated by the quagmire of cars that he vowed then and there to do a trip where a traffic jam was an abstraction. During his 2,000-mile solo paddle from Grenada to Puerto Rico, he paddled in 25-foot seas, was repeatedly bumped by sharks as long as his 17-foot Klepper kayak, and endured a 110-mile, 28-hour open-water crossing. (A trifle, in my view, compared to the Lincoln Tunnel at rush hour.) While his trip was dangerous — the open ocean is the province of experts, mad dogs, and Englishmen — he spent the next few weeks eating tropical fruit on pristine islands, which sounded quite bearable.

Later that same summer of 1994, I met Verlen Kruger, a retired plumber and father of nine from Lansing, Michigan, and truly a legend in his own time. At the age of 66, Verlen set out on his first jaunt, a 7,000-mile, 176-day trip across Canada from Montreal to the Bering Sea. Later, he paddled 21,000 miles from the top of Alaska to the tip of South America. Kruger, who is now in his 80s, has logged nearly 100,000 miles on the water and is still going strong. In 2001, Kruger at 79 and a partner won a nonstop race down the 2,500-mile-long Mississippi River — a mere side trip for a guy who's done two trips longer than 20,000 miles.

Listening to these two adventurous guys in the summer of 1994 flipped a switch in my landlubber brain. For my bike tours, I always searched the map for scenic secondary roads. But it had never occurred to me that rivers were, as Verlen said, America's first highways and that you could paddle all the way across the country if you didn't mind some hideous portages along the way. So I did it. The following spring I drove a one-way rental car from New York to Montana, left it at an agency in Helena, bummed a ride south from a friend to the Clark Canyon Dam on the Beaverhead River close to the Continental Divide, unloaded my boat on the banks of the Beaverhead, and launched what turned out to be a 103-day paddle back home.

The circuitous point here is that once you start exploring the rivers and creeks around your home, there's no telling where you may go. My friend Nels, a mountain climber and professional photographer, paddled for years on the Rock River, a tributary of the Mississippi, which flowed a few blocks from his childhood home. One spring he and his dad spent two weeks paddling the length of the 310-mile river. When that trip ended at the Mississippi, it was inevitable that he start thinking about paddling all 2,500 miles down to New Orleans. And paddle he did, becoming at 21 the youngest person to travel the length of the river solo.

PERCHANCE TO DREAM: TRIP PLANNING

Trips, long and short, usually start with the same idea. "I want to go somewhere in a boat." But where? Unless you're visited by an apparition, subscribe to *Paddler, Canoe & Kayak* or *Sea Kayaker* magazines, or date a professional river guide, odds are that you're not sure where to turn your amorphous idea into a reality. The following are just a few ways to get started.

STUDY A MAP

Look at a river or lake in your vicinity. (Cut costs and start by exploring something close to home.) Where does it begin and end? Are there lengthy portages, dams, or huge reservoirs to negotiate? What kind of terrain surrounds it? Is it wide? Narrow? Swampy? What are the best places to put in and take out? When I thought about paddling across the country, I read maps the way a hungry man would a diner menu. While I focused on the Missouri, it was impossible not to speculate about the Yellowstone and North Platte Rivers. Reading maps with this mindset connects you to a web of waterways that should fill you with possibilities. If it doesn't, you're probably not all that eager to travel by small boat for days at a time. If not, don't worry. There's plenty of other fun to be had in a kayak.

GO TO THE LIBRARY

One of the sources of my fascination with river travel started when my mother read Mark Twain's *The Adventures of Huck Finn* to my brother and me when we were kids. Since then I've read countless adventure travel books about and by people who have undertaken incredible self-propelled journeys on major waters. Three of my favorite paddling books are Joe Kane's *Running the Amazon,* Paul Theroux's *The Happy Isles of Oceania,* and Don Starkell's *Paddling the Amazon: The Ultimate 12,000-Mile Canoe Adventure.* Browse the adventure travel section of a bookstore or library and your creative trip-planning juices are bound to start flowing. Verlen Kruger says of Samuel de Champlain and the French fur traders who followed him across some of the wildest waters of North America: "Ever since I started reading about those early explorers they've been my heroes. What we do for fun, they did for a living."

THINK SMALL

Lots of people flirt with the idea of doing an epic trip, but logistics (read fear) get in the way. Comments like "I don't have the time or money or know-how . . ." are common. But there's no need to think in grand terms. A "small" trip can be very rewarding. Instead of paddling the length of a great river, find out about its most beautiful or accessible section and just paddle that. I've done thoroughly satisfying two- and three- day jaunts in the Adirondack Mountains that were adventurous yet relaxing. When our daughter was two years old, my wife and I put in a canoe on the Raquette River outside the town of Saranac Lake, New York. We had originally planned on covering 30 or 40 miles over the weekend. But our nonlinear tyke had other ideas. We ended up covering roughly eight miles in two days. But because we'd traveled to a beautiful place in a boat we had a great time; well, at least we had *some* pleasure, which is about all you hope for when you're traveling in the company of a teething two-year-old.

TALK TO PEOPLE

Paddlers all have stories to tell. Clubs, Web sites, friends, the UPS man are all potential sources of information. To check out information on canoe and kayak trails, go to *www.nativetrails.org.* Before I started on my Missouri River trip, I talked to two guys who had paddled the entire river and badgered them for the cold hard facts. Today, I have a long list of potential trips — from paddling through the Florida Keys to an exploration of the Apostle Islands on Lake Superior, to a trip down the upper Connecticut river that runs near my brother's house in southern Vermont — that were inspired by the tall tales of fellow paddlers.

If you've never paddled before, if you're in poor physical condition, or if you loathe camping, at this point you should flip back to chapter 1. Ditto if you love to paddle but hate to plan. There are plenty of adventure travel companies that lead kayak trips all over the world. My first experience in a kayak was a guided trip in Florida's Ten Thousand Islands. If you pay close attention and pepper your guide with questions, you can learn a lot. But with someone else doing the thinking, it's all too easy to sit back and enjoy the scenery and company without paying much attention to what it really takes to get from point A to B.

But let's assume that you have been paddling a while and want to head out on your own. I am also going to presume that you've now got a boat, an assortment of paddling and camping gear, adequate self-rescue and camping skills, and a trip in mind. If you fall short on the above criteria (as I did), you can still bash ahead (as I did), and you'll probably survive (as I did). But it does make sense to learn to walk before you run, or at least to tie your own shoelaces.

So how do you get to the water with the right equipment, companions, and state of mind?

PLAN YOUR ROUTE

Whether you're going on an epic journey or a weekend excursion, good maps are a must, the indispensable tools for planning a trip. And the more detailed the better. If you have an outdoor store in your area with detailed maps of your intended route, go there and ask lots of questions. If such a resource is unavailable locally, go to *www.usgs.gov* to order United States Geological Survey maps of your entire route. In addition, this site will give you an idea of the water level on all streams and rivers with gauging stations. This is important because if the river you want to paddle on in July is barely deep enough to wet your paddle, you'll need to make an adjustment.

LOGISTICS

How long will it take to cover the route? How much time do you have? How will you get to the water? If you drive yourself there, where will you leave your car? If your schedule is flexible, then duration of the trip isn't crucial. But if your schedule is not flexible, you may need to build in some extra days for contingencies like headwinds, low water, or illness. Again, the more information you have, the better you'll be able to estimate the time you'll need to cover the distance you want. If you're traveling a known waterway like the Maine Island Trail, call a local out-door store or find a locally focused guidebook with detailed information to get as many facts as you can. If it's a river that takes you far from civilization, prepare for the unexpected and build more extra time into your trip.

GEAR

Having the right equipment can make the difference between a good trip and a frightful survival story. As I've previously mentioned, I set out on the Missouri with a sleeping bag rated only to 32°F, and nearly froze during an unusual (but not unheard of) spring storm. Knowing the range of conditions you may encounter is crucial. Once you figure out what kinds of gear you'll need for those conditions, don't assume Mother Nature will cooperate just because you're out there looking for nautical bliss. Skimp on gear and the odds are high that you'll need what you left behind.

BUCKS

Unless you plan on staying at motels every night, the biggest expenses are 1. equipment, 2. food, 3. getting to and from the venue, especially if it's far from home. During my two-and-a-half months on the Missouri, I spent close to $2,500, including buying new gear and renting a car to get to Montana. Once you're on the water, you can expect to spend $10 to $30 a day on chow, depending on your appetite, accessibility of stores, and your long-term tolerance for Rice-a-Roni.

COMPANIONS

I've done most of my trips alone. While traveling solo presents a few more inherent risks, I enjoy the freedom of being able to go when and how far I want to based on how I feel. Solo travelers don't have to put off trips because no one else was available. I actually enjoy what Adirondack adventurer George Washington Sears called "the blessed calm of lonely places." When I crave human contact, it's relatively easy to seek out the company of strangers. If you do plan on going with a mate, make sure you are compatible. First, do a few day trips together. Discuss what kind of food you plan to take and, more important, the proposed pace and goals. A mileage hound traveling with a sniff-the-roses type is a combustible combination. If you're on the same page before you start, you're likely to be simpatico on and off the water. If you do go with a partner, definitely take two boats instead of one tandem — in kayaking circles a.k.a. "a divorce boat" unless you've already traveled together. That way if you tire of each other you can paddle separately during the day and then reconvene in the evening.

GETTING WET

To make the abstract real, let's look at three trips I have taken, for a real sense of what to take, how to pack, and the other nitty-gritty details involved in making a trip come to fruition. I'm assuming that you've got a complete set of maps, enough food (or enough money to buy it along the way), and a plan for getting to and from the place you intend to paddle.

TRIP ONE: MELLOW

The Raquette River, New York's second-longest river, is an intimate, dark, narrow waterway that winds its way north from Raquette Lake to the Saint Lawrence River through a maze of alder-studded islands. Though I'd paddled it a few times at race pace, my goal this weekend in August was to do some mellow canoe camping with my wife, Beth, and daughter, Willa.

Equipped with a good map, the "Adirondack Canoe Map," and a sturdy Kevlar rental canoe, we drove to a marked put-in outside the town of Saranac Lake.

Here's what we took:

Three sleeping bags and sleeping bag pads secured in two heavy-duty zip-top garbage bags

A two-person Eureka tent (double bagged)

Jugs of water and food for three days: dried fruit, candy bars, canned tuna fish, peanut butter and jelly, hot chocolate powder, macaroni and cheese

Small propane-fueled camp stove

One cooking pot, three spoons, and three plastic mugs

Clothes for paddling, including Gore-Tex raincoats and fleece jackets in case of cold weather. We each took a pair of shoes for wearing in the boat and an extra pair for hanging around camp.

Medical kit, including matches and a lighter (see page 48)

Beer

Spare paddles

Flashlight

A highly flexible attitude. Traveling with a small child, I've found that trying to cover a lot of distance is a recipe for frustration. Expect to go slow, enjoy the scenery, and you'll be rewarded.

Once you're on the riverbank, it is time to unload the car and pack the canoe. Don't rush. It is important to put all your clothes and other don't-get-wet items in waterproof bags (so-called "dry bags" do work well) as well as to pay careful attention to balancing the gear fore and aft. When I'm in a kayak, I worry less about gear floating away in the event I capsize because the gear is stowed in hatches. In an open canoe, however, it is important to make sure everything that could float away is secured. (Bungee cords and/or elastic cords work well.) When our canoe is packed, I have a silent word with the local river gods, make sure my car key is in a safe place, get in, and start paddling with a destination in mind.

kayak with touring gear — getting packed

On this trip, we paddled down the Raquette for a few hours, found an idyllic lean-to site to pitch our tent in, set up camp, and watched as Willa pulled imaginary fish from the water. That night we were rewarded for our effort with a sky full of brilliant stars, something we don't see often in Brooklyn. The following day, we got up late, ate a big breakfast, paddled some more, then turned and headed back upstream by sunset.

An hour later, we were back in town eating Mexican food.

TRIP TWO: MEDIUM MELLOW

Early trappers called the 90-mile route of interconnected lakes and rivers from Old Forge to Saranac Lake "the old highway of the Adirondacks." I call it one of the prettiest three- to four-day paddles in the East. While I raced on this route a couple of times — feeling visually content, but physically in distress — this particular long weekend in October my friend Mike (also a competitive kayaker) and I decided to do it in a leisurely manner, in which pleasure, not pain, reigned supreme. Because we planned on paddling 20 to 30 miles a day and because there were a bunch of long portages, we planned on traveling light.

We drove Mike's van with our kayaks on top and parked off the side of the road at a convenient put-in in Old Forge. Had we two vehicles, we could have shuttled one to our proposed take out. Since we didn't, we planned to hitchhike back to the car at the end of the trip.

Basically, we took much of the same essential gear I took on my overnight jaunt with my wife and daughter. But with two kayaks we split the communal gear in half. The principal difference was accounting for the weather. Since we were paddling in October, an iffy month weather-wise in northern New York, we brought warmer clothes and top-quality rain gear.

Our "extras" included:

Wool hat

Synthetic gloves (for out-of-boat use)

Pogies (in-boat use)

Compass

Warm socks

Head lamp (leaves your hands free to paddle)

Coffee (lots of it)

Spray skirts

All-in-one tool for repairs

Freeze-dried foods like "Teriyaki Chicken with Rice" and "Turkey Tetrazzini." They are light, easy to carry, and, after you've paddled six hours that day, rather tasty.

Water purifier

Rain jacket (easily accessible whenever we paddled) and pants

Thick-soled water shoes for walking along the trails

Camp booties to keep feet warm at night

Medical kit (see page 48)

It rained often on our trip, but when we arrived in Saranac Lake three days later, we were both thoroughly satisfied. I lost the coin toss, donned a backpack with food and water, and headed to the road in search of a ride. My hitching trick, other than smiling beatifically with my thumb extended, is to carry a canoe paddle, a symbol that plenty of people in the Adirondacks know, means that I paddled my backside off and parked my car a long way upstream. My first ride took me 40 miles up the road. The next car stopped before I could say Ralph Waldo Emerson two dozen times fast. In fact, the friendly couple (paddlers both) went out of their way to drop me at Mike's van.

TRIP THREE: HARD-CORE

Whether you're planning to do a biggie like the Mississippi River or Intracoastal Waterway from Maine to Key West, or a semi-biggie like the 100-mile Everglades Wilderness Waterway, any trip requiring more than a week exposed to the elements requires great endurance, mental tenacity, improvisational know-how, and flexibility. It's important to note that on a great river, the only thing you can control is your attitude. After his epic trip across northern Canada, Alan Kesselheim said, "Did we make mistakes? Of course. Were we lucky? Hell yes. Did things go according to plan? Only loosely. But 420 days later we had put a remarkable trip in our canoe wake, a trip that changed our lives."

My three biggest mistakes prior to starting my paddle down the Missouri was that I lacked the proper cold-weather gear (nearly a fatal error); failed to bring a water purifier, which meant I had to schlep a two-gallon jug of water around; and, because I was anxious about covering the distance, I didn't pace myself well.

Success on a long journey requires more preparation, greater physical fitness, and an ability to paddle effectively in a variety of conditions. If you haven't paddled in volatile weather or in big water before, or had to press on past the point of exhaustion, odds are that you will when you venture far from home. But that's part of the excitement, as long as you're prepared.

While unloading the boat was painless, it typically took me 30 to 40 minutes to set up camp. Packing up, no matter how fast I worked, took me an hour or more, depending on how lethargic I felt. Know this: Initially, fitting all my gear in the kayak seemed a daunting task. After a week I dialed in a packing system and knew exactly what went where and how. There's no other way but trial and error to make it work.

Were I to do that long journey again, I would bring:

Appropriately-rated sleeping bag. Sleep is your savior, so make sure you get a good bag. For a trip that starts in Montana in the spring, I'd go with a -25°F bag.

Neoprene Farmer John

Neoprene gloves to wear under my pogies

Down coat

Mountaineering gloves or mittens

Neoprene socks to wear under rubber boots

Water purifier

Axe or **saw**

AM/FM Radio

Medical kit (see page 48)

Lightweight bent-shaft canoe paddle. Not only is it a great spare in case you damage or lose your kayak blade, it's a good alternative to its double-bladed brethren when you want to use different muscles.

An ambitious trip is the product of inspiration. Certainly the more prepared and experienced you are, the less likely you are to, say, blow a hole in your tent with your propane stove, forget to tie up your boat at the end of the day, or try to cross a huge reservoir in a howling head wind. But you will mess up somewhere, somehow; that's why the key to a successful expedition is *passion*. If you're enchanted by the power of water and eager to see how you respond to the challenges of living outdoors, you are exactly where you should be, even if the river gods see fit to rain on your trip.

relaxing after setting up camp

——

GREAT KAYAK DESTINATIONS

As you've probably guessed by now, I like to paddle — oceans, rivers, lakes, flooded basements, mud puddles. Prior to writing this book, I spent five years driving around America climbing the highest point in each of the 50 states for a book called *To The Top*. While my focus during that peripatetic road trip was vertical, every time I passed a body of water I pondered aloud about the paddling possibilities. (I finally stopped when my partner, photographer Nels Akerlund, noted that I was driving him insane.) Regardless, the point remains that once you begin to think like a kayak crazy the paddling opportunities are endless because viable waterways are everywhere.

What follows is a roundup of some paddling places that I've enjoyed and a few that I'm eager to try. When you go to try them, remember that when heading out onto a new body of water, always bring along a good map and compass, and enough information about the weather and conditions to ensure that your first foray is a safe one.

EAST COAST

Adirondack Park, New York. At six million acres, Adirondack Park in upstate New York is a paddler's paradise with 2,759 lakes and ponds and 1,500 miles of rivers and streams. Given its combination of navigable waterways, forest and mountains, the park is wild and scenic. You could speed-read the terrain in September by entering the three-day, 90-mile Adirondack Canoe Classic, which follows the original "Highway of the Adirondacks"— or tackle it on your own schedule. Once traveled by settlers and guides, this route follows interconnected lakes and rivers and requires several portages. The route starts at the town of Old Forge on the Fulton Chain of Lakes and heads east to Raquette Lake, along the Raquette River into Middle, Upper and Lower Saranac Lakes and finishes on Lake Flower in the sleepy town of Saranac Lake, in the High Peaks region. I've done the race three times and done it as a pleasure cruise once. Unless you're training for an Ironman Triathlon (or traveling with a masseuse), don't try to paddle it in three days; even five or six days is still a hard-core adventure. Of course you could pick just one section, set up camp, and explore it thoroughly over one long weekend.

The Island Trail, Maine. The Maine Island Trail, a 325-mile island-dotted stretch along the Atlantic coast from Portland to Machias, is a sea-kayaker's premier East Coast destination. There are protected bays and inlets, lots of big open water, breaking surf, and enough birds and wildlife to absorb a naturalist for a lifetime. But remember, as one guide says, "Keep a weather eye out, eh?" Fog is a big factor in these parts so be skilled with your compass. (A GPS is a great help in this environment.) My favorite part of the trail starts around Acadia National Park's Mount Desert Island. There are plenty of guide services in the area that will help you avoid the lobster pots — on the water, that is.

Honorable Mention. Having paddled down the **Hudson River** from Albany to New York City three times, I'm partial to this powerful river, especially around West Point, roughly 40 miles north of the Big Apple. There, the river narrows down and takes a "where'd it go?" bend, creating what looks like a collision of river, cliffs and foliage. The one thing you don't want to collide with is the commercial barges that silently rule the water in the shadow of the U.S. Military Academy. Two good put-ins for this paddle are Hudson Highlands State Park upriver and across from West Point, and just to the south of the state park in the quaint old town of Cold Spring in Putnam County.

A hectic urban — but rewarding — paddle is to circumnavigate the island of Manhattan via the Hudson, East, and Harlem Rivers. It's about a 30-mile trip, and unless you're really strong and experienced you'll need to study the tide charts. The short stretch called "Hell Gate," where the East River meets Long Island Sound, has ripping currents and enough old shipwrecks to warrant extreme caution. Still, I know of no better views of Manhattan than from the seat of a kayak cruising offshore.

I'm also a big fan of the **Connecticut River,** particularly of its upper reaches where it forms the border between Vermont and New Hampshire. Another favorite is the little-known **Upper Ashuelot River** in Keene, New Hampshire. Also, hit the **Charles River,** 30 miles or so upriver from downtown Boston—it's great paddling, given that you're on a river so close to a major metropolis.

SOUTH

During a road trip five years ago, a friend and I drove from New York to Florida, stopping frequently to paddle along the way. In Georgia, we drove to **Tybee Island,** a National Wildlife Refuge just east of Savannah, and enjoyed a few hours of frolicking with dolphins in the Atlantic. (Prior to this paddle I'd never frolicked, but dolphins can have that effect.) Farther south, near the Florida/Georgia border, we explored the spooky, protected waters of **Okefenokee Swamp**. We also spent some hours paddling offshore in the ocean and among the islands along the **Intracoastal Waterway,** then drove across Florida to **Sanibel Island** on the Gulf Coast outside of Fort Myers. In 1993, I spent a glorious week of kayak-camping in the **Ten Thousand Islands** in the Gulf of Mexico just off the Everglades. The classic route there is the 100-mile **Wilderness Waterway** from Flamingo to Everglades City. Finally, three of my favorite rivers in the Sunshine State, all less than an hour's drive from Gainesville in north-central Florida, are the **Santa Fe, Ichetucknee** and **Suwannee.** If you can hit only one, opt for the "Ich"; it is the most intimate, and surely must rank among America's prettiest little rivers.

MIDWEST

Boundary Waters Canoe Area, Minnesota. The BWCA may well be the best flatwater paddling venue in the country, containing more than 1,000 lakes and several river systems. Paddlers willing to tread over the portages in the interior of this vast wilderness will find enough solitude even for a recalcitrant monk. To get to the area, head up highway 61 from Duluth towards Grand Marais on the shore of Lake Superior, then follow the Gunflint Trail (aka Highway 12), a 56-mile two-lane road, and stop where the pavement ends. It's worth the drive. For a rugged three- or four-day trip, put in on Seagull Lake at the end of the Gunflint Trail and head west to Little Saganaga, one of the more remote lakes in the million-plus acres of this northwoods wilderness. Along the way you'll paddle though stunningly clear, hard-to-pronounce lakes like Ogishkemuncie, Agamok and Gabimichigami. There are nine portages in all, varying from 300 to 1,000 yards. Some are steep, but unlike the voyageurs — those French trappers who pioneered over these same trails — you won't be shouldering bales of furs. You will be likely to see moose, black bear and, if you're lucky like me, a glimpse of the northern lights. Before heading home, stop in Ely, an old mining town, for a beer and mooseburger. After a bunch of days in the bush, a cold one is nearly required.

Honorable Mention. The Wisconsin River, a tributary of the Mississippi, is a mostly sedate, intimate river of modest reputation but surprising beauty. The two neatest sections are the start at the Michigan/Wisconsin border near a sleepy hamlet called Land O'Lakes. On my first day on the narrow, twisting upper section, I put in there and exited six satisfying hours later at Eagle River, the snowmobile capital of the world. Another great stretch of the river lies farther south between the towns of Wisconsin Rapids and Portage. Here, when you enter a narrow channel called the upper Dells, you'll be surrounded by 100-foot high striated sandstone cliffs rising out of the deep, iced-tea-colored water. The Winnebago called this area Neehahkecoonahera — "the place where the rocks strike together." By any name it's worth a visit. Islands, gulches, canyons, and bluffs make up the state's greatest rock show, courtesy of the glacier that sculpted the Potsdam sandstone over the course of 30,000 years. One legend has it that when Paul Bunyan lay down to rest in the Dells, his head made the Sugar Bowl while his heels dug out caverns called — get this — "Paul Bunyan's Heels." The best put-in is just below the Castle Rock Dam near White Creek on the east side of the river. When you arrive at the Dells, you'll know it.

WEST

As I've detailed in prior pages, I paddled the length of the 2,500-mile **Missouri River,** getting my feet literally and figuratively wet as an expedition paddler. (My feet dried out about two months after I got home.) To me, the most spectacular stretch of the 800 miles that flows through Montana is the Wild & Scenic section in the east-central part of the state. This part of the Missouri, one of the few areas still unchanged from the days of the Lewis & Clark 1804-1806 expedition, prompted Meriwether Lewis to write several pages about the "seens [sic] of visionary inchantment." Wind-eroded white cliffs dropped straight into the river. Cooing swallows, racing in and out of holes in the sandstone, turned the towering cliffs into a giant speaker system. Some of the rocks looked like outsized mushrooms, others like melted castles, or grand tabletops. "Geology here," wrote one Missouri river buff, "is as current as a newspaper and far more sensational." Sensational or not, William Clark was correct when he said, "I do not think it can ever be settled." The weather is harsh and the land unforgiving, and since "there ain't no services in these parts" you'll need to be self-sufficient. (If you don't bring your own water, bring a purifying system.) If you head south from Havre, Montana on Route 234, you'll need to negotiate a mostly dirt road to put in on the north side of the river. A great take-out, roughly 50 miles downstream, is the James Kipp Recreation Area Boat Ramp. There is plenty of current on this section of river so you can just float if you like. Camping spots abound on the banks and there's enough scenery to leave you as "inchanted" as Lewis & Clark were nearly 200 years ago.

WAY WEST

Hawaii. Often when I discuss the paddling opportunities in Hawaii I turn into a blathering idiot. I've spent time on Oahu, the Big Island,

Maui, Kauai, and Molokai, and each has such spectacular water and scenery that you begin to understand why the ancient Polynesians revered it and why the enthusiasts do the same today. My favorite place to paddle on Oahu is **Kailua Bay** on the southeast coast. Rent one of the plastic sit-on-top boats and paddle out to the **Mokelukas Islands,** twin islands roughly 30 minutes offshore, that provide one of the best picnic spots on the planet. On Kauai, the sheer verdant cliffs on **Na Pali Coast** have no rival, but make sure you go with a guide who knows his way around the cliffs since the seas there can be treacherous if the swell is up. In short, get to the South Pacific, get wet and you'll be back for more.

Alaska. While the paddling possibilities in Hawaii and Alaska are as different as, say, pineapple and potatoes, there's one powerful similarity: both offer enough water to occupy you for a lifetime and both offer stunning scenery. I spent just a week paddling with my family among the bald eagles and curious sea otters south of Homer in a remote inlet in **Kachemak Bay,** but it was long enough to understand why people say Alaska offers the best sea-kayaking in the world.

Glacier Bay on the southeast coast is probably the most famous area and, no doubt, it is amazing. But virtually anywhere on the southern coast will be "the most beautiful place you've paddled" if you've never been to Alaska before. Of course, the Alaskan waters are killer cold, so much so that you must be skilled enough to roll your kayak or be able to right it and get back in within five minutes. (Go, of course, with a partner since paddling alone here is foolish.) In addition, the rivers in the interior of the state are swift, remote, and cold so only go with an outfitter or highly experienced friends.

MAJOR KAYAK MANUFACTURERS

Ace Kayak
Tomandglo Ltd.
315-685-6291
www.acekayak.com

Aqua Fusion
866-882-2663
www.aquafusion.com

Azul Kayaks
Voodoo Technology
514-931-0366
www.azulkayaks.com

Bell Canoe Works
866-437-0081
www.bellcanoe.com

Betsie Bay Kayak
231-352-7774
www.bbkayak.com

Bliss-Stick
+64-6-388-1445
www.bliss-stick.com

Boreal Design
418-878-3099
www.borealdesign.com

Caillou Boats
www.caillouboats.com

Chesapeake Light Craft
410-267-0137
www.clcboats.com

ClearWater Design Canoes & Kayaks
613-471-1005
www.clearwaterdesignboats.com

Cobra Kayaks
310-327-9216
www.cobrakayaks.com

DAG
+33-475-367-327
www.dag-kayak.com

Dagger Kayaks
864-859-7518
www.dagger.com

Discover
Seaward Kayaks
800-595-9755
www.discoverkayaks.com

Easy Rider Canoe & Kayak Co.
425-228-3633
www.easyriderkayaks.com

Eddyline Kayaks
360-757-2300
www.eddyline.com

Englehart Productions
EPI Kayaks
216-641-5337
www.emc-epi.com

Epic Kayaks
866-438-3742
www.epickayaks.com

Eskimo USA
866-405-4293
www.eskimo-kayaks.com

Feathercraft Products
888-681-8437
www.feathercraft.com

Folbot, Inc.
800-533-5099
www.folbot.com

Fujita North America
866-915-2925
http://fujitana.com

Great Canadian Canoe
800-982-2663
www.greatcanadian.com

Great River Outfitters
401-667-2670
www.grokayaks.com

Guillemot Kayaks
860-659-8847
www.guillemot-kayaks.com

Heritage Kayaks
336-454-8385
www.heritagekayaks.com

Hobie Cat
800-462-4349
www.hobiecat.com

Hurricane Aqua Sports
www.hurricaneaquasports.com

Impex Kayaks
MidCanada Fiberglass
828-225-5201
www.impexkayak.com

Island Waveskis
800-777-2613
www.waveski.com

J. K. Inc.
Canyak
641-847-2151
www.canyak.com

Kajak Sport
Global Outfitters
617-834-5623
www.gokajaksport.com

Kiwi Clear Kayaks
Plastitech Products
800-545-2925
www.clearkayak.com

Klepper USA
800-500-2404
www.klepperusa.com

Kruger Canoes
231-266-2089
www.krugercanoes.com

Laughing Loon Canoes & Kayaks
207-549-3531
www.laughingloon.com

Lincoln Canoe & Kayak
207-865-0455
www.canoesandkayaks.com

LiquidLogic Kayaks
828-698-5778
www.liquidlogickayaks.com

Long Haul Products
970-856-3662
www.longhaulfoldingkayaks.com

Mariner Kayaks
206-367-2831
www.marinerkayaks.com

Millbrook Boats
603-239-4633
www.millbrookboats.com

Morley Cedar Canoes
406-886-2242

NC Kayaks
Novus Composites, Inc.
888-441-8582
www.nckayaks.com

Necky Kayaks
Johnson Outdoors Inc.
800-852-9257
www.necky.com

Nigel Foster Kayaks
Seward Kayaks
800-595-9755
www.fosterkayaks.com

Nimbus Kayaks
Rainforest Designs
604-467-9932
www.nimbuskayaks.com

Northwest Kayaks
Outdoor Synergy
800-648-8908
www.nwkayaks.com

Ocean Kayak
800-852-9257
www.oceankayak.com

Old Town Canoe Co.
Johnson Outdoors
800-343-1555
www.oldtowncanoe.com

Old Tymers Pleasure Craft
518-781-3372
www.oldetymers.com

P. & H. Sea Kayaks U.S.
828-254-1101
www.phseakayaks.com

Pakboats
888-863-9500
www.pakboats.com

Pelican International
888-669-6960
www.pelican-intl.com

Perception Kayaks
864-859-7518
www.perceptionkayaks.com

Persson Manufacturing
860-767-3303
www.perssonmfg.com

Phoenix Poke Boats
800-354-0190
www.pokeboat.com

PouchBoats
802-649-2555
www.pouchboats.com

Pyranha US
828-254-1101
www.pyranha.com

QCC Kayaks
888-794-3887
www.qcckayaks.com

Riot Kayaks
514-931-0366
www.riotkayaks.com

Scott Canoe
MidCanada Fiberglass Ltd.
705-647-6549
www.scottcanoe.com

SeaDog Boats
414-614-4158
www.seadogboats.com

Seavivor Folding Boats
847-297-5953
www.seavivor.com

Seaward Kayaks Manufacturing
800-595-9755
www.seawardkayaks.com

SEDA
800-322-7332
www.sedakayak.com

Simon River Sports
905-420-2085
www.simonriversports.com

Splashdance
850-678-1637
www.splashdance.com

Squeedunk Kayaks
218-682-2110
www.squeedunk.com

Stewart River Boatworks
218-834-2506
www.stewartriver.com

Stillwater Boats
301-774-5737
www.stillwaterboats.com

Superior Kayaks
920-732-4602
www.superiorkayaks.com

Swift Canoe & Kayak
800-661-1429
http://swiftcanoe.com

Tideline Kayaks
858-405-0652
http://eteamz.active.com/paddleshop

Toquenatch Creek Cedar Kayaks
604-483-7762
www.cedar-strip.com

Twogood Kayaks Hawaii
808-262-5656
www.twogoodkayaks.com

Valhalla Surf Ski Products
858-569-1395
http://eteamz.active.com/ValhallaSurfSkis

Venture Sport
561-395-1376
www.venturesport.com

Walden Kayaks
Earth Friendly Kayaks
508-992-4144
www.newwaldenkayaks.com

Wavesport Kayaks
864-859-7518
www.wavesport.com

**Wenonah Canoe and
Current Designs Kayaks**
507-454-5430
www.wenonah.com

West Side Boat Shop
716-434-5755
www.westsideboatshop.com

Wilderness Systems
864-859-7518
www.wildernesssystems.com

Wildwasser Sport
303-444-2336
www.wildnet.com

Woodstrip Watercraft Co.
610-326-9282
http://woodstrip.wcha.org

Accessories, 47–48, 48
Adirondack Park, 116–17
Alaska, 121
All-in-one tool, 48

Back brace, 63, 63–64
Back paddling, 65
Beam sea, 62
Bearing, 97–99, 98
Big boat encounters,
    79–81, 80
Boats. See Kayaks
Bomber roll, 8, 15, 81
Booties, 43, 43
Boundary Waters Canoe
    Area, 118–19
Brace entry, 53, 53–54
Bracing, 59–64, 60–61, 63
Breaking waves, 56–58
Breathing, 74

C1/2s (racing canoes), 11
Calm, staying, 72–74, 73
Capsizing, 8, 73, 81–87,
    82–84, 86
Catch, 25–26, 26
Cell phones, 72
Charts, 93, 94
Clothing, 42–46, 43–45,
    46
Combing, 51, 51
Compass, 70, 71, 96–99,
    98
Connecticut River, 118
Costs
    of gear, 33–34
    of touring, 108
Crab walk, 55, 55–56, 58

Declination, 97
Destinations, 116–21

Downwind, 63
Draw stroke, 29, 29–30
Dry bags, 47
Dry launch, 51–52, 51–53
Dry suits, 45
Duct tape, 48

East coast trips, 116–18
Eskimo roll, 8, 15, 81

Feathered paddles, 40, 41
Fingerless mittens (pogies),
    45, 45
Following sea, 63
Forward stroke, 23, 23–27,
    25–26
"Free speed," 19

Gear. See also Kayaks
    basics, 33–48, 43–45,
        46, 47–48
    navigation, 96–100, 98
    survival, 70–72, 71, 77,
        79
Getting in, 50–58, 51–55
Getting out, 58–59, 59
Glacier Bay, 121
Global Positioning System
    (GPS), 72, 99–100

Hatches, 36
Hats, 44
Hawaiian trips, 120–21
High brace, 62
High-performance sea
    kayaks, 38, 39
Hip flick, 61, 62
Hudson River, 117
Hugging shore, 78, 79
Hydration system, 47–48

Ichetucknee River, 118
Intracoastal Waterway, 118
Island Trail, 117

Jackets, 44, 70, 71
Jet ski encounters, 81

K1/2/4s (racing kayaks),
    13–14, 14, 36
Kachemak Bay, 121
Kailua Bay, 121
Kayaking, 49–65. See also
    Gear; Navigation;
    Safety; Touring
    bracing, 59–64, 60–61,
        63
    destinations, 116–21
    getting out, 58–59, 59
    landing in breaking sea,
        64–65
    launching, 50–58,
        51–55
    power paddling, 17–31,
        19–20, 22–23, 25–26,
        28–29, 65
    rewards of, 1–6
Kayaks. See also Paddles
    basics, 7–15, 10, 13–15
    choosing, 35–40, 38
    manufacturers, 122–25

Landing in breaking sea,
    64–65
Launching, 50–58, 51–55
Layered clothing, 43, 44
Life jackets, 47, 70, 71
Lost, being, 90–91

Manufacturers, 122–25
Maps, 74–75, 93–96, 94,
    105, 107

Marine maps, 93, 94
Medical kit, 48
Midwestern trips, 118–19
Missouri River, 120
Mokelukas Islands, 121

Na Pali Coast, 121
Navigation
    basics, 89–100, 94, 98
    compass, 70, 71, 96–99,
        98
    Global Positioning Sys-
        tem, 72, 99–100
    maps, 74–75, 93–96,
        94, 105, 107
Nightime paddling, 80

OC1/6s (outrigger
    canoes), 11, 12
Okefenokee Swamp, 118

Paddle float, 85–87, 86
Paddle grip, 23, 24
Paddles. See also Power
        paddling
    basics, 40, 40–42, 42
    leash, 47, 79
    loosing, 78, 79
Personal flotation device
    (PFD), 47, 70, 71
Planning trips, 104–9
Pogies (fingerless mittens),
    45, 45
Power paddling, 17–31,
    19–20, 22–23, 25–26,
    28–29. See also Brac-
    ing
Power (pull) phase of pad-
    dling, 26, 27
Pressure breathing, 74

Racing canoes, 11
Racing kayaks, 13–14, 14,
    36

Rain jacket, 45
Reach vs. rotation, 24–25,
    25
Recovery, 26, 27–31,
    28–29
Recreational canoes, 10, 10
Recreational kayaks, 13,
    37, 38, 39
Relaxation techniques, 73,
    73–74
Reverse paddling, 30–31
Rewards of kayaking, 1–6
Rolled kayaks, 8, 73,
    81–87, 82–84, 86
Rough water, 19–21, 20
Route planning, 107
Rudders, 36

Safety. See also Navigation
    basics, 67–87, 71, 73,
        78, 80, 82–84, 86
    Eskimo roll, 8, 15, 81
Sanibel Island, 118
Sante Fe River, 118
Scale of maps, 93–94
Sculling brace, 62–63
Sea kayaks, 12–13, 13, 36,
    37, 38, 39
Shelter, 75
Shipping lanes, 80
"Shortie Farmer John," 44,
    44, 77
Shorts, 43
Side brace, 60, 60–63
Sitting entry, 52, 52–53
Six-man outrigger canoes
    (OC6), 11
Small trips, 106
Solo trips, 108–9
Southern trips, 118
Splash gear, 45
Spray skirt, 47, 47
Standing entry, 51, 51–52
Starboard, 25

Straddle entry, 54, 54
Sunglasses, 45
"Surf ski," 14
Survival gear, 70–72, 71
Suwannee River, 118
Sweep strokes, 28–29,
    28–30

Ten Thousand Islands,
    118
Throw rope, 48
Topographic maps, 93, 94,
    94, 107
Touring, 101–15, 111,
    114. See also Naviga-
    tion
Touring cruiser, 38, 39
Touring kayaks, 12–13, 13,
    36, 37, 38, 39
Two-person kayaks, 39
Tybee Island, 118
Tying kayaks, 77–78

Used kayaks, 39–40
USGS maps, 93, 94, 94,
    107

Water launch, 53–54,
    53–54
Waves, 61, 61–62, 63,
    63–64
Weather, 42, 46, 108
Western trips, 120–20
Wet suits, 44, 44, 77
Whistles, 47, 70, 71
White-water kayaks,
    14–15, 15
Wilderness Waterway, 118
Wind, 75–77
Winged paddles, 42, 42
Wisconsin River, 119

ABOUT THE AUTHOR

When Joe Glickman is not out paddling, he's back home in Brooklyn, New York, writing books and magazine articles. A two-time member of the United States National Marathon Kayak Team, Glickman has paddled and raced on the waters of several continents and in countries ranging from Thailand to Tahiti, from South Africa to the U.S.A. He has paddled the length of several major U.S. rivers, and raced from Chicago to New York.

Glickman's articles, on kayaking and other outdoor sports, have appeared in *The New York Times* and *The Washington Post, The Village Voice, Outside, Men's Journal, National Geographic Adventure, Inside Sports, US, The Paddler, Sea Kayaker,* and many other publications. His books include *That's Not The Way it Was: (Almost) Everything They Told you About Sports Is Wrong* (Hyperion) with Allen Barra; *Our Wisconsin River — Border to Border* (Pamacheyon Publishing); *The Idiot's Guide to Rock Climbing, The Idiot's Guide to Weight Training* and *The Idiot's Guide to Short Workouts* (Alpha Books). He also contributed to *A Brooklyn State of Mind* (Workman Publishing).

While Glickman is a self-confessed "kayak crazy," he has taken occasional breaks from paddling to explore the limits in other demanding sports: bicycling from coast to coast and from Portland, Oregon to Los Alamos, New Mexico. He's also a technical mountain climber and recently summited Mount McKinley and has reached the highest point in all 50 states — and written a book called *To The Top* (North Woods Press).

Also in Storey's *Quiet Sports* series:

The Hiking Companion by Michael W. Robbins (ISBN 1-58017-429-9).